HOW OLD ARE YOU?

UNDER 16? 16-40? OVER 40?

Is this your first pregnancy?	Yes___	No___
Multiple births expected?	Yes___	No___
Previous miscarriage or stillbirth?	Yes___	No___
Exposure to rubella?	Yes___	No___
Rh-negative blood?	Yes___	No___

Have you ever had:

heart disease?	Yes___	No___
diabetes?	Yes___	No___
kidney disease?	Yes___	No___
venereal disease?	Yes___	No___

Is there a history of genetic problems (Tay-Sachs disease, sickle-cell anemia, Down's syndrome) in the family?	Yes___	No___
Do you smoke heavily?	Yes___	No___
drink heavily?	Yes___	No___
use drugs frequently?	Yes___	No___

A "Yes" to any of these means you should see your doctor. However:

"Today, any woman, old or young, in good health has every reason to expect a safe and happy delivery. I welcome the appearance of *Pregnancy After 35*."

—Howard Berk, M.D.,
From the *Foreword*

Carole Spearin McCauley

Pregnancy After 35

FOREWORD BY DR. HOWARD BERK

A KANGAROO BOOK
PUBLISHED BY POCKET BOOKS NEW YORK

The author thanks these publishers for permission to quote passages from the following: From *Pregnancy: The Psychological Experience* by Arthur and Libby Colman. Copyright © 1971 by Herder and Herder, Inc. Reprinted by permission of The Seabury Press. From *The Male Machine* by Mark Feigen Fasteau. Copyright © 1974 by Mark Fasteau. Used with permission of McGraw-Hill Book Company. From *Thank You, Dr. Lamaze* by Marjorie Karmel. Copyright © 1959 by Marjorie Karmel. Reprinted by permission of J.B. Lippincott Company. From *Childbirth With Hypnosis,* by William S. Kroger and Jules Steinberg. Copyright © 1961 by William S. Kroger and Jules Steinberg. Reprinted by permission of Doubleday & Company, Inc. From *Preparing for Parenthood: Understanding Feelings About Pregnancy, Childbirth and Your Baby* by Lee Salk. Copyright © 1974 by Lee Salk. Reprinted by permission of David McKay Co., Inc. From *Psychological Aspects of a First Pregnancy* by Pauline Shereshefsky and Leon Yarrow. Copyright © 1973 by Raven Press Books, Ltd. Reprinted by permission of Raven Books, New York City. From the book *Childbirth Without Pain* by Dr. Pierre Vellay, translated by Denise Lloyd. Copyright © 1959, 1960 by E.P. Dutton & Co., Inc. and George Allen & Unwin Ltd. Reprinted by permission of the publishers, E.P. Dutton & Co., Inc.

POCKET BOOKS, a Simon & Schuster division of
GULF & WESTERN CORPORATION
1230 Avenue of the Americas, New York, N.Y. 10020

Copyright © 1976 by Carole Spearin McCauley

Published by arrangement with E. P. Dutton and Co., Inc.
Library of Congress Catalog Card Number: 76-4958

ISBN: 0-671-82275-6

First Pocket Books printing August, 1978

Trademarks registered in the United States and other countries.

Printed in the U.S.A.

Contents

FOREWORD

THE ERA HAS PASSED WHEN A WOMAN HAD to choose between motherhood and/or "working" at a job, career, profession "out in the world." Contemporary women want *both* lives and a society that recognizes this fact and assembles services to make it possible. The woman over 35 may be leading the way in these combined roles: education and job involvement in her twenties, followed by a choice to have a child or children at a later age than has been the traditional pattern.

Much attention has been paid to younger mothers, especially teen-agers. We needed a popular book to help the older couple.

I appreciated the opportunity to read this book "for medical accuracy." It is thorough, well researched, and well written. I also was pleased to note the attention the author pays to fathering and to single parenting.

The book contains the latest information on those genetic, psychological, and medical topics that are of special interest to women or couples over 35 planning a baby or already expecting a first or later child. The author interviewed or corresponded with over a hundred individuals—older parents, physicians, psychologists, midwives, and members of groups concerned with bettering pregnancy, genetic counseling, and birth services and practices for American couples.

This book will help you ask the right questions to secure the best medical care and birth education offered in
your community. The health-insurance chapter will answer your questions on financing such services. No matter
what your age, if you are pregnant, you can put to use
the material given here on such topics as nutrition, the
management of your emotions during and after pregnancy,
and the newest birth methods.

At any age the psychosomatic aspect of pregnancy is an
interaction among four important Ps—a woman's parity
(the number of previous births she has had), the pelvis,
the perineum (the tissue around the vagina), and her
psychology. These factors also help determine the quality
of her childbirth experience. Today, any woman, old or
young, in good health has every reason to expect a safe
and happy delivery.

I welcome the appearance of *Pregnancy After 35*. I
learned from it and believe you will, also.

> Howard Berk, M.D.
> Beth Israel Medical Center
> New York City

INTRODUCTION

"WHAT IS THE MOST IMPORTANT THING YOU learned during this pregnancy?" I asked of a Maryland woman, Dee. She was 45 and her husband 42 when they had a first baby.

She answered, "The importance of the love of a woman and a man creating a new love."

I began this book with the idea that pregnancy and birth are private events, different for each woman or couple. Yet I rapidly got involved in the sociology—and politics—of contemporary birth methods and education, related to older parents. In these days of Women's Liberation, changing sex roles, economic recession, medical care, and malpractice-insurance reforms, I inevitably met with crossfire, such as the right-to-lifers versus pro-abortionists, medical reformers versus establishment physicians, women desperate that I recognize the trauma of infertility versus those desperate that I heed world overpopulation.

One leader in the gynecology self-help movement (whose aims I respect) attacked me. "You're *not* writing another lousy, male authority-oriented book!" She's right; nearly 97 percent of 16,000 U.S. obstetrician-gynecologists are men. However, a skillful, humane doctor—or midwife—is ideally so beyond his or her sex. Gender should indicate biology, not humanity.

Some crossfire involved physicians about colleagues.

Some doctors believe, for example, that the genetic counseling process, especially for older women, saves babies; others believe it encourages abortion. Another example: When I merely mentioned Dr. Landrum Shettles' name (of sex selection infamy, pp. 79–82) to another physician, he announced, "Dr. Shettles is crazy, and his method is nonsense." It seems that whatever idea one doesn't personally like is "the latest fad done by quacks."

The split that most intrigued and confused me was that between people who consider birth and parenting one of life's peak periods ("I felt alive in every part of me!" or "Holding our baby seconds after my wife gave birth was the most thrilling moment of my life") and those who consider it a drag on time, money, sleep, whatever goods might be better employed for one's own use. "We wanted babies, but my God, who needs kids?" If ambivalence is a normal part of pregnancy, it is certainly so with parenthood.

Many years ago Queen Christina of Sweden said, "To believe all is weakness; to believe nothing is stupidity." To demystify this welter of viewpoints, I informed myself through medical-journal articles, interviews, questionnaires, ads inserted in two magazines. I attended a series of meetings of a public-health group planning a special New York City program of medical care for pregnant women over 35. I also talked with unmarried mothers and with some who chose abortion.

How does all this affect *you* as an expectant or new parent? Your goal is to have and raise a baby safely, which is challenge enough. I have aimed at a blend of material and data that is medically, psychologically sound, yet humanly interesting.

For better or worse, you won't find this book a diatribe against the medical establishment, the school system, "national priorities," or the Pentagon. It is for people who try hard at what is the essence of parenting as well as living —stretching bodies, minds, and hearts far enough to include that very new idea, the next generation.

Pregnancy
After 35

CHAPTER 1

How Old Is "Older"?

REGARDING PREGNANCY AND BIRTH FOR women over 35 and their babies, medical opinion is surprisingly un-unanimous about who or what constitutes "high risk." Beyond certain deterrents to pregnancy (diabetes, extreme obesity, breast tumor, kidney disease, epilepsy, high blood pressure, sever mental and marital problems), *age alone need not be a factor.*

The extreme conservative position, of course, says that any woman pregnant over 35 is automatically high risk to herself and baby, regardless of physical condition.

The liberal, optimistic view holds that only one in ten middle-aged mothers should be considered high risk (from some already diagnosed disease or abnormality) and that 60 to 80 percent of maternal and infant complications arise during labor and delivery, regardless of age, with no prior warning. The optimistic opinion, held by enlightened physicians and most nurse-midwives, for example, emphasizes pregnancy as a normal phenomenon, not an illness, and that even high-risk patients can be adequately managed with proper diet, birth training, and attitude.

Dr. Sid Sharzer is a Los Angeles obstetrician who has

delivered over 6,000 babies. He believes that contemporary women are healthier than their foremothers because they eat a better diet, especially more protein. They are also more conscious of the need for regular exercise and medical exams, including prenatal care.

Sally, a labor-room nurse in my community, told me, "In nursing school, we were taught about difficult labors, fourteen hours or more. Here I see seven-hour labors with a first baby and shorter for second or later babies. I think modern women are just in better shape."

What does medical literature reveal for the different age groups: women giving birth after 35, 40, even 45?

The most recent study I located typifies others from the last 20 years in viewpoint and statistics. Reported in *Obstetrics-Gynecology News* (February 1, 1975), it quotes Dr. Steven Craig Johnson on his research with 26,000 deliveries at the University of Iowa Hospital, Iowa City, between 1962 and 1972. Of these, 293 (1 percent) occurred in women who were 40 or over at time of delivery. (This is well below the national figure of 3 percent—about 100,000 births yearly; in England it is 2.5 percent. For New York State, including New York City, during 1973 nearly 4,500 women over 40 had babies.)

Pregnancy and birth were normal in two-thirds of these patients studied, but many had more than one complication. Twenty percent of pregnancies encountered coincidental medical problems such as hypertension (34 patients), diabetes, kidney disease, rheumatic and coronary diseases of the heart, cancers of the breast and cervix. While pregnancy did not cause any of these conditions, it probably aggravated them.

The rate of Caesarean sections performed was 13.6 percent—twice the rate for other patients. Remember, however, that older women are often scheduled for Caesareans automatically on the theory that their tissues and pelvic structures are more fibrous, less elastic, therefore less capable of normal delivery than the younger woman's body. One obstetrician, Dr. Edward Waters, wrote, "Pelvic types unfavorable for normal vaginal delivery occur four times as often in the elderly group." And Dr. Sharzer believes that, compared with other parts of a woman's body, the arteries in the uterus age and harden faster; in his view, the "older uterus" is less able to cope with nourishing the fetus and disposing of its wastes.

How about the babies in Dr. Johnson's study of mothers over 40?

Ninety-one percent of babies were born alive; the perinatal ("around birth") mortality rate was 9 percent. The usual rate for this hospital is 1.8 to 2.6 percent. Twenty infants (6.8 percent, about twice the national average of 3 to 4 percent for women over 40) had congenital abnormalities, mostly Down's syndrome and heart disease.

Dr. Johnson concludes: "It is at times difficult to state whether age or parity [total number of births per women] go hand in hand or are specifically responsible for these complications. . . . There is a definite high risk for both the mother and infant in patients over the age of 40."

I interviewed several women like Joan and Alice (Chapters 7 and 14) who safely bore a first child when they were over 40. Actress Arlene Dahl had her third child at 41. Her other children were 10 and 14 at the time. In midpregnancy her worries were those of most women—how to cope with an expected baby's needs, to continue her work obligations, to stay attractive to herself and husband. Later she wrote: "I now do stretch and bend exercises daily, walk a lot, and stick to a high protein diet which includes one dessert daily (fruit, Jell-O, or low-cal pudding). Fortunately I package my own protein diet snacks, gelatin capsules, and vitamin-mineral tablets, which are available at most Sears stores. Without the diet snacks—I take two before each meal—I'm sure I would have gained 50 pounds during the last three ravenous months of pregnancy alone.

"None of my apprehensions was exactly groundless. But they didn't materialize either. I found pregnancy at 40 more of a challenge, physically, physiologically, and psychologically, than my other two in my twenties and thirties. And whereas I had taken my earlier pregnancies largely for granted, this one filled me with continuous wonderment and gratitude.

"Best of all, I really did—and still do—feel younger, mainly because I identified with younger women, their body processes, their joys and problems."

What of the woman over 35 instead of 40?

Women aged 35 to 39 produce 7 percent of U.S. births

annually—some 225,000 babies. During 1973 in New York State, including New York City, over 18,000 women between 35 and 39 had babies.

Here's the largest study I found, done by Drs. A. C. Soumplis and D. E. Lolis at the Alexandra State and University Maternity Hospital, Greece (*Internal Surgery* 52: 340–44, 1969). It analyzes records of 1,574 "elderly women" (1,364 of them aged 35 to 39) among a total of 58,851 deliveries during the period 1955–63. This amounts to 2.67 percent of total births—one woman of each 37. An impressive 22 sets of twins were born— nearly 14 percent of births compared with the usual rate of 1.2 percent (11.5 births—fraternal and identical twinning combined—per 1,000 births for white women); 739 women (46.9 percent) delivered spontaneously, as opposed to delivery by forceps. The average labor was 4 hours, 6 minutes—very brief—using what the doctors called "accelerated painless labor," which is the Lamaze method probably speeded by pitocin, a labor-inducing drug.

Toxemia (about 10 percent) and fibroid tumors of the uterus (about 3 percent) were the most often encountered maternal health problems. The Caesarean rate, despite use of the Lamaze method and minimal anesthesia (anesthesia retards efficient functioning of uterine muscles), was an elevated 25.4 percent. Of these 1,574 women, 6 died (.38 percent), and about 9 percent suffered postpartum illnesses. The combined fetal and neonatal mortality rate was 5.32 percent.

The doctors concluded that age of patients (their oldest was 47) "is directly related to the incidence of labor complications, as well as to the type of delivery."

Not all doctors consider older women to be high risk. As Joan (p. 85) mentions, her doctor "was a bit nervous about my age (40) but otherwise treated me routinely." Dr. Sherwin Kaufman of New York University School of Medicine writes, "Despite the added risk, there is no real reason to dissuade a woman in this age group from conceiving if she wants a baby." Discussing 502 women ("Pregnancy at Age 40 and Over," *Obstetrics and Gynecology* 17:194, 1961), Dr. Lewis Posner, Harlem Hospital Center, New York, writes:

The incidence of malpresentation [abnormal presentation of fetus] was low. Eighty percent of the labors were completed within 8 hours. The incidence of serious obstetric complications was low. There appears to be no relation between the age of the mother and the viability of her infant. The woman aged 40 or over, despite her tendency to systemic disease, has a good chance of bearing a live infant at term.

At least one doctor considers the *baby*, rather than the mother or her age, as the patient to whom the label "high risk" should apply. After studying five years of records (1968–72) plus a five-year follow-up of infants born to 127 "elderly patients," Dr. Ian Morrison of Winnipeg, Canada, wrote, ". . . granted careful prenatal care, maternal mortality rates in the elderly primigravida [woman over 35 pregnant for the first time] group compare favorably with the figures for the younger age groups and that the label 'high risk' in a modern obstetric context applies to the fetus." ("The Elderly Primigravida," *American Journal of Obstetrics and Gynecology* 121:465–70, 1975.)

Here is a mixed viewpoint by Dr. E. A. J. Alment, Northampton Hospital Group, England, on women over 35 bearing their first child: "The elderly primigravida is a high risk case and should be booked for delivery in a specialist obstetric unit" (*Practitioner* 204:371–76, 1970). He adds, however:

With the recent trend toward more active management [mothers awake for delivery] it is difficult to draw any conclusion about the effect of maternal age on the duration of labor. . . . The elderly primigravida is exposed to high risks, some of which can be reduced by efficient antenatal care with ready resort to specialist advice, careful postnatal attendance, the avoidance of both prematurity and postmaturity, delivery in a specialist unit, and early resort to operative decision in the face of any adverse obstetric factors.

The elderly primigravida, after all, has made a long journey; she deserves to arrive safely.

Dr. Alment—to his credit—does elaborate on the emotional needs of the older pregnant woman:

> Whilst she is likely to be better informed about pregnancy than her younger counterpart, her awareness can deprive her of the protection of blissful ignorance which is part of the inborn optimism of the young primigravida. [!] Fear of foetal malformation . . . is especially true of the elderly primigravida. Her encounter in large antenatal clinics with a vast majority of younger patients . . . can give her a sense of inadequacy, of late arrival, and make her withdrawn and sensitive, less able to communicate her needs. Thus she will especially need tact, time, and privacy to help her in the dialogue with doctors and midwives which is an essential aspect of antenatal care.

The "psychology of pregnancy" (Chapters 9 and 10) is a little- or misunderstood topic often neglected in prenatal care. Obstetricians are increasingly aware of the need to consult in psychosomatic matters with psychologists and psychiatrists. However, people in the women's movement, worried about the stereotypes surrounding woman-as-ill-patient (of any kind), have mixed feelings about this.

My interviewees, upon discovering their pregnancies, had reactions ranging from "delighted" to "shocked." One Boston mother, pregnant after her marriage at 38 and having quit her job of 20 years, wrote me, "Everyone seemed to harp on my age and its possible negative effect on my health, the baby's health, my ability to cope with motherhood and present lack of a career."

Susan Catania is a Chicago mother of 6 children; her fifth, Amy, was born when Ms. Catania was about 35. Amy aroused considerable notice and some resentment because Susan Catania is a representative to the Illinois State Legislature. Since Susan believes in breast-feeding, she fed Amy on the job to the notice of news reporters. Her jealous male colleagues considered Amy's presence "a publicity stunt" because state legislators "just don't get publicized unless they are indicted or convicted." Ms. Catania manages her life with the aid of a cooperative husband and the flexible hours allowed state legislators. She also pays two-thirds of her salary to employ two housekeepers. When she appeared on NBC TV, toddler Amy happily crawled around the podium, oblivious of cameras and Barbara Walters. At the time of this interview Ms. Catania was expecting another child. She is an amazing woman.

Finally, what of pregnancy over maternal age 45?

Here are results from a study of 26 mothers who delivered from 1957 to 1971 at Strong Memorial Hospital, Rochester, New York. The analysis was done by Dr. Robert J. Sokol and associates, reported in *American Journal of Obstetrics and Gynecology* (119:6, 767–74, 1974), and titled "Computer Diagnosis of Labor Progression in the Very Elderly Gravida."

Some of his conclusions are:

The woman over 45 tends to be generally healthy. There are no important differences in antepartum and postpartum complications when compared to younger patients of similar parity.

Advanced obstetrical age is not associated with labor prolongation but the risk of abnormal labor progression [due mostly to malposition] is significantly increased. Fifty percent of the group experienced an abnormal labor (vs. 16% of the younger control group).

Anesthesia in both groups was minimal. Approximately 85% of patients in both groups received no more than nitrous oxide [gas] and a pudendal or local block. No caudal [spinal] anesthesia was used. Three study and four control patients received general anesthesia for vaginal delivery.

Lastly, the father of one healthy infant was 75 years old!

Dr. Albert Hayden, a Teaneck, New Jersey, obstetrician, is an optimist on the question of late pregnancy. "It's more of a pleasure to take care of a woman having her first baby at 40 because it is a very exciting time of her life. She makes a good patient, and the reason is that she has had 40 years to mature." After studying 600

mothers over 40, he concluded that while there are a few
more problems, "these women do seek prenatal care.
They are probably attended more carefully, make more
visits to the obstetrician than the younger age group." Dr.
Hayden also admits a personal bias. "My mother was 47
years old when I was born, so I am all for women over
40 having babies."

Dee C., who was 45 at the birth of her child, wrote me,
"There certainly seems to be a feeling that after 35,
you're too old. But I know different, and I like it this
way!"

On this matter of maturity, one 38-year-old mother
describes the rewards of what she calls her "second family." "At 20 you take having kids for granted; at my
age you count your blessings. You may not have the
stamina you once had, but you're more relaxed and patient. You've learned that youngsters are with you for only
a limited time, and you make the most of it."

In later chapters I'll mention more studies and statistics
on pregnancy and birth for older couples. These include
factors such as race, which can determine quality of nutrition and care; multiparity ("many births"), which is the
older couple's propensity for twinning and tripletting; and
the new field of genetic counseling.

If you are fortunate, you will experience late pregnancy
with a minimum of raised eyebrows from friends, parents,
your other children, even your obstetrician. In my interviewing, I found it common for a woman or couple,
having surmounted various doubts and problems, to rejoice finally that they did choose to continue a pregnancy.

A woman with an unusually difficult history is Mrs.
Emmanuel Ben-Amos, who was 40 at the birth of her
son, Omri. A native of Czechoslovakia, she was one of
80 children to survive the concentration camp at Ausch-
witz. She is now a packaging designer in Manhattan.
Of her parenting fears and joys she said, "If I had been
20, perhaps I might not have had all the fears I did have.
I developed great insecurity even though I was quite secure about everything else. I was so scared at first that I
wouldn't let anyone handle him, and I worried about
making mistakes. The first child is more difficult for an
older woman. She has no one to turn to."

She added, however, "I've never enjoyed anything

more. I was a frustrated, bitter female before. Having a baby puts value on life."

If you are 35 or over and expecting a child, birth and parenting will be as safe, successful, even as exciting an adventure as you care to make them. And to do this, you must choose your medical care and birth education thoughtfully, locate people whose aims and approach correspond with yours. A conservative medical approach can and does prevent trouble in some high-risk cases. However, as we have seen, only a minority of woman over 35 are automatically high risk.

Well-known pediatrician and author T. Berry Brazleton, in *Be a Healthy Mother, Have a Healthy Baby* (Rodale Press, 1973), has this comment:

> In our medicated society we have eradicated some of the pain and anxiety, but I'm afraid we have eradicated more of the excitement and joy. Pregnancy, labor, and delivery are thought of as essentially a disease in the United States. As a result, the anxiety and fear and pain are medically treated as if they were evil and destructive symptoms of the "condition" rather than positive forces that mobilize a woman for an awesome, prodigious and usually enormously rewarding experience—the birth of a child.

CHAPTER 2

Questions and Answers

"MOTHERHOOD IS A DEMANDING AND COM-
plex career for which most of us are given no preparation." Joanne, 38, New Jersey mother of children aged
1 and 2.

"Fatherhood is loving and taking care of a family."
Forty-three-year-old Long Island father of five, including
a new baby.

In doing this book, I talked with many older parents.
Others wrote me about their personal experiences.

Some women were pregnant at the time; others were
eager to discuss their recent delivery experience (good
and bad). A few were hoping for a child soon despite
infertility or other problems. Some had recently ended a
pregnancy through abortion. Each group (pregnant or
new mother, desiring or not desiring a child) contained
both single and married women. To accept and raise a
child without a partner is a challenging, but increasingly
accepted, lifestyle. The unmarried woman who might
previously have adopted a baby is now having her own
because, as one of my interviewees, a businesswoman,

said, "I was raised with much love. I wanted to give love to someone. Now I have someone to receive it."

I sent out questionnaires that covered certain basics, such as the woman's reaction to discovering she was pregnant, her treatment by her doctor and hospital personnel, whether she had received genetic counseling or birth education, any contrast between early and late stages of her current or last pregnancy, whether she was covered by medical insurance, the effect of the baby on the couple's work and family life and their attitude toward parenthood in general. What I sought was not statistical data but personal opinions on the emotions and experiences of pregnancy and birth.

Here are just a few of my questions and some of the answers they elicited. Their human variety is evident.

The pregnant body is . . . "funny!" . . . "ugly!" . . . "rather marvelous" . . . "interesting" . . . "beautiful in a spiritual and emotional way" . . . "big!"

What was your husband's reaction when you first learned you were pregnant? "Shocked." "Delighted." "He was positively mortified and for a long time refused to acknowledge the very apparent fact." "Very happy." "Ecstatic." "He said, 'Guess it's about time.' " "He said, 'How do *you* feel? You're the one who does most of the work.' " "Delighted—but not surprised."

Maternity clothes . . . "I like" . . . "are generally made to make you look worse" . . . "For me, saris create no problems." . . . "are divine, comfortable, and beautiful—ever looked in Lady Madonna on Madison Avenue?" . . . "usually much larger than needed and more feminine. I don't buy them." . . . "are attractive and comfortable but often too youthful."

One Maryland woman, when asked the most important thing she'd learned through parenting, replied: "Priorities —how to set them and the patience to live with those chosen."

My oldest respondent, Susan Hale, from the state of Washington, is now 57. She was 40 when her fourth child, Cindy, was born. Her first child was then 16, her husband 49. Susan wrote me:

"I was *theoretically* against another baby. The idea of a new pregnancy was devastating. My first reaction to pregnancy was distress. My husband was supportive but not enthused. I did get the name of an illegal abortionist, but I didn't have the nerve to go through with it. I had no more trouble with childbirth after I read Read's book, *Childbirth Without Fear*. I enjoyed all my pregnancies except that this last one did bring varicose veins and pushed my weight up permanently.

"Our 'old age child' is now 17. She has always been a joy. She is our best-adjusted child. Older women who had late daughters were genuinely enthused about my new child, and now I know what they mean. Cindy is not the bright, magnetic child my other daughter was. But she is sweet, serene, and understanding. She seems proud of her parents and not a bit worried that we are a generation older than those of most of her friends. Her older siblings have all been fond of her and she of them."

During all these years Susan also helped earn the family living as farmer's wife, newspaper columnist, and schoolteacher. She also ran for a political office.

Susan's nearly 35 years of successful parenting reveal some basic truths about the experience. There are biologic and psychological constants within the total process, but to these each woman or couple makes its own response. And this varies from moment to moment, year to year, with love, dismay, hate, ambivalence, joy alternating or mixing in a challenging, even bewildering succession.

Sue F., 40, of Baldwin, N. Y., whose 17-month-old Patti is her fifth child, described what happened when she first informed her teen-agers about the coming event. "They were all a little stunned, then excited and happy. Janet cried with joy. John, 17, shook his father's hand and said, 'Congratulations, Dad!' "

Although Sue worried during pregnancy about possible abnormality, Patti turned out lively and healthy. "I've done a lot of things differently with this child. I'm more relaxed, and I'm older and smarter. I have the sense to go to bed when I'm tired. Also, our income has risen with our age, and we can better afford this child." Sue was an elementary schoolteacher; her husband is a municipal bond salesman.

"This baby has brought such joy to our lives. But I had forgotten how messy kids can be. My kitchen floor is a disaster area when she eats. I steel myself not to watch, then clean up afterward."

One response I received reads like fiction: "A 37-year-old woman, divorced and mother of two, undergoes an unwanted pregnancy and travels to a city halfway around the world rather than opt for an abortion. Her children, ex-husband, and the father of the baby all cooperated in the venture. No one else knows the true circumstances of the tour except a few good friends and one family member, whose help became necessary to carry off the whole thing. . . . This story is mine. . . ."

Joyce, now 50 and my oldest correspondent, is also a recent mother. She was 46 the day her daughter Anne was born. The mother of 8, she already has grand-children who now play with her preschooler. Her husband "enjoyed the good-natured ribbing of friends, and father-hood at 47 is considered quite a feat in our society."

"This was our eighth child (7 daughters, 1 son), and we aren't even Catholic! Abortion had been considered briefly, but in vew of the fact that two miscarriages had been followed by mild depression, it seemed unwise—and it wasn't that easily obtained in our area five years ago. Besides, we were financially and physically able to handle a new baby. The specter of a handicapped child loomed in my mind often. I tried not to dwell on it, but it seemed almost every time I went out, I would see a child with some disability."

The birth and postpartum period proceeded well except for a "dam of tears" that broke when her husband and teen-age daughter telephoned from a business trip.

"We weathered the colic. I joined Weight Watchers and lost the 27 pounds that made me feel really dowdy when I sat in the waiting room of the pediatrics clinic with all those willowy young things with their first or sec-ond child. I was able to get away fairly often for a few hours or several days . . . but it wasn't until our church had a weekend of spiritual renewal when she was about 6 months old, that I was able to really accept this mir-acle child, love her, and cope with my mixed feelings of resentment and blessing. . . .

"Thanks to much encouragement and support from my husband and family, and the good fortune of a live-in baby sitter, I managed to get a master's degree in teach-ing home economics during this period. Then we moved. Although it has necessitated some difficult adjustments, it also opened up new challenges, including an interesting part-time job for me. Our full-time help returned to the area we left, so I'm struggling with child-care needs again. . . . The fact remains that the pleasure of being a grandmother twice is somewhat overshadowed by the ongoing responsibilities of my own preschooler, though the three little ones have great fun when they're together.

"Anne and her daddy have had a great time this year exploring interesting places—the zoo, museum, the Horicon Marsh where the geese stop on their way south—and then sharing their discoveries with family and friends. Her zest for life is an inspiration and blessing for us all. We're very grateful that this bonus child is a beautiful, bright, well-adjusted little girl, but also trying to face realistically the frustrations that are a part of parenting a preschooler after 50."

A few women, overwhelmed with marital and/or financial problems, were honest about their dilemmas. "My first and last child was born exactly two weeks before my thirty-fifth birthday. Having been told for 15 years by various M.D.s that I was incapable of conceiving, I was extremely surprised when my gyn. gave me the word. . . . It isn't that I wouldn't like another child, but as my husband is so neurotic/psychotic, that is enough to squelch even so much as a passing thought on going through the whole performance again. I don't need the aggravation. . . ."

Another woman, 46, described herself as "the menopausal mother of a 3-year-old."

My general conclusion is that women and couples of 35 and over who have *chosen* new parenthood (when they could have secured abortion) are mature, motivated people who are coping well with all their various roles and lives.

Do you wonder which of my questions provoked the greatest variety of answers? This one:

If men could get pregnant
"we'd have no overpopulation problems."
"abortion would be a sacrament."
"women would lose their specialty."
"they wouldn't think it was so great that I could."
"they'd enjoy it."

"—forget it."

"they couldn't stand the pain."

"they would learn a lot!"

"there would be honesty and understanding about sex."

CHAPTER 3

Are You High Risk? Choosing a Hospital and Doctor

ALTHOUGH SOME GYNECOLOGISTS CONSIDER you already "elderly" at 35, you are not rare. Couples over 35 account for 10 percent of U.S. births annually—nearly 325,000 babies. If you are *feeling* elderly as you read this, you should know about the oldest new mothers on record, documented in England. The ladies were a spry 80 and 63 years old for the births about 1700 and 1882. The latter woman had even produced twins when she was 50! In the U.S. a few years ago (1957) a Baltimore woman had a girl and a boy when she was 51 and 53.

Assuming you are interested in a doctor and hospital delivery, what kind of treatment you will get is not totally decided by the doctor or hospital. It is *your choice* as a couple—to educate yourselves, to locate care suitable to your needs, finances, personality, judgment.

Here's a questionnaire to help you determine your needs. If you're pregnant and find yourself in any of these categories, many obstetricians will consider your case high risk and want to monitor your progress in various ways.

How old are you? Under 16 or over 40 are high risk.
Which birth will this be for you?
    Fifth or later
    First child to woman 35 or older
    Twins or triplets expected
What is your medical history?
    Previous miscarriage or stillbirth
    Previous Caesarean
    Previous toxemia of pregnancy
    Previous premature birth
    Previous baby with birth weight over 9 or under 5 1/2 pounds
    Previous multiple pregnancy
    Bleeding during previous pregnancies
    Rubella (German measles infection). You are protected from this through antibodies if you have already had it.
    Toxoplasmosis. See p. 100. It is also thought that individuals who contract this are immune to it in the future.
    Known bone deformities, especially of the pelvis.
    Too small pelvis.
    Incompetent cervix. Mouth of the uterus does not remain sufficiently closed to contain developing fetus and membranes.
    Rh factor. Rh incompatibility occurs when wife is Rh negative, husband is Rh positive and has transmitted his positive factor to fetus. See pp. 100–101. The damaging effects can now be largely prevented by immunizing the woman with a Rho-GAM injection, provided sensitization has not occurred from a previous incompatible transfusion or a previous pregnancy when Rho-GAM was not administered.
Have you had—?
    Anemia
    Heart or circulatory disease
    High blood pressure
    Diabetes
    Kidney disease
    Malnutrition or obesity
    Thyroid problems (over- or underactive)
    Urinary tract infection
    Emotional instability
    Prolonged severe stress

Tuberculosis
Syphilis or gonorrhea
Genetic problem in either of your families?
   Previous child, sibling, or ancestor with defects such
      as Down's syndrome, Tay-Sachs disease, sickle cell
      anemia
*Do you smoke or drink heavily? Use drugs of any kind
frequently?*

Some women over 35 may have none of these problems. Others may have suffered some combination—high
blood pressure, ulcer, or thyroid condition, for example—
now controlled through medication. Chronic problems
such as extreme obesity or diabetes definitely classify you
as high risk.
Where should you deliver?
   The largest single factor modifying the experience of
labor and delivery in our culture—for good or ill—is the
medical setting, including medical personnel. If you feel
or are told you are high risk, consider the following while
choosing an obstetrician and hospital.
   1. If you're new in a community, or if your previous
birth experiences were less than satisfactory, *begin with
the hospital.* If you choose the doctor first, you are locked
into the hospital in which he is a staff member or treats
patients.
   Some people—husbands and wives—may feel that a
woman spends only five days of the whole nine months
in the hospital. What difference does it make? They all
give the same care, don't they? Luckily or unfortunately,
depending on your viewpoint, they do not.
   Joan (pp. 85–86) was highly satisfied with hospital policies that encouraged parent participation and breast-
feeding. Alice (pp. 150–151), lacking both time and tran-
quillity before her son's birth, was not; she was chagrined
when she discovered the rigid policy for Caesarean patients plus the general discouragement of breast-feeding.
Joan and Jay chose their doctor through the hospital; Alice
chose hers in ignorance of its restrictions.
   2. *Try to attend a prenatal class,* film, or talk at one of
the hospitals in your area. If a tour of labor and delivery
rooms or nursery, including facilities for premature babies, is offered, examine the situation, meet the staff and
nurses. Are they friendly, willing to spend a few moments

explaining their work, answering reasonable questions? Or are they rushed and nervous, considering you an intruder? You are not an intruder. In a few weeks or months they may be supervising your care. If this is a public hospital, your taxes help pay their salaries.

3. *Ask about policies for Lamaze patients* if this method interests you. Will labor and delivery happen in the same room, or will you be moved at the last minute? What is the hospital's policy on father participation in labor and delivery? Its policy on breast- and/or bottle feeding? On visits to mother and newborn by family members, including the baby's brothers and sisters? On administering drugs, solutions, injections, examinations? Which of these are routinely given by nurses to laboring mothers? Which must be ordered by your doctor?

If you're an average healthy woman who hasn't been hospitalized since you had your tonsils out at age 5, or since you last gave birth, hospitals can be disconcerting places. Nurses and aides appear constantly in your room with various pills, liquids, thermometers, injections, forms, taking urine and blood samples, taping your wedding ring down, removing your eyeglasses—procedures that may seem dubious or disorienting and to which nurses may give no answers unless you ask beforehand.

4. If your community possesses more than one hospital, *consider the merits of small and large institutions.* For our purposes, a small hospital is one that handles less than 500 deliveries per year. An experienced obstetric nurse remarks, "Small hospitals in small towns do a better job for the average uncomplicated case. The mother knows the nurses. The doctor knows the father. The father can come and go."

That is, while a small institution has rules and standards like any other, it will probably also allow small gestures of friendliness that may be vital to your sanity. Nurses with whom you're well acquainted will be more willing to discuss aspects of your care, what is necessary and why. If they know your visitors, your husband's presence in the room won't disturb them, your guests won't be checked every 15 minutes for their permit cards, etc.

On the other hand, here is what Dr. Ben Peckham, chief of gynecology-obstetrics at the University of Wisconsin, says: "The real difficulty with the small hospital is that they're not really set to take care of even the average patient. The average patient who was perfectly uncomplicated before she went into labor can get complicated awfully fast."

Dr. Howard Berk, an obstetrician at Beth Israel Medical Center, New York City, corroborates this viewpoint. "Facilities to help high-risk patients and babies should be available, although numbers of women may not need them. Most difficulties that occur during labor do not give previous warning. In fact, 'average' is a retrospective label only. No patient, older or younger, should really consider herself average before the event."

In 1967 the ACOG (American College of Obstetricians and Gynecologists) published a report on American hospitals correlating efficiency with factors such as size, annual number of deliveries, presence of teaching staff. The report noted that 25 percent of U.S. hospitals required more than 40 minutes to prepare for Caesarean surgery; 43 percent needed more than 30 minutes' notice to administer blood; 30 percent needed more than 4 hours to prepare for exchange transfusions.

Other common deficiences noted were the absence of a separate recovery room for use after delivery, lack of continuous observation of mother and baby for one hour after birth, and failure to do complete observation of the newborn.

There are currently 7,500 hospitals in the U.S. treating nearly 1 1/2 million in-patients (for all health problems) daily.

5. If you are high risk, *investigate facilities at one of the new "perinatal centers."* Most centers are the maternity wings and attached nurseries of large hospitals affiliated with medical schools. Some famous ones are Yale Medical Center, New Haven, Conn.; Boston Lying-In Hospital; Columbia Presbyterian Medical Center, New York City; Wisconsin Perinatal Center, Madison; University of Southern California Medical Center, Los Angeles.

All these centers (each may deliver some 5,000 babies per year) provide intensive care for laboring women and for the high-risk babies that high-risk mothers can produce. Support services, available within minutes, include laboratories, blood bank, hematology and radiology equipment, and personnel on duty around the clock. In addition to obstetrician-gynecologists and anesthesiologists, the personnel includes neonatalogists, who are doctors for the newborn, and nurse-specialists (counseling care), nurse-clinicians (physical care), and nurse-midwives. There are also pediatricians, social workers, cytologists, and genetic counselors plus their supportive technicians and equipment.

The value of such a center is not only the lives it saves but that a couple's whole prenatal experience and birth education can occur in one location. A woman's physical exams, Lamaze classes, and training in baby care can take place there. The same nurse-clinician or midwife who does prenatal exams may continue with the couple through actual labor and delivery. Perinatal centers also have outreach programs of public health education and review of medical data on a regional or city-wide basis.

6. If you can't reach a perinatal center but must choose between a hospital approved for doctors' residency or internship training and one without, *choose the hospital that helps train doctors.* The equipment and care are apt to be better with 24-hour-a-day facilities. Such a hospital must also meet requirements of the American College of Surgeons and American College of Obstetricians and Gynecologists. Investigate the teaching hospital in your area.

CHOOSING YOUR DOCTOR

1. *Talk with other parents,* especially with nurses or people who know doctors well. Learn their recommendations. For instance, when I asked a medical switchboard operator why she chose Dr. X for her gynecology surgery, she replied, "Well, he's an older man, dependable. When his patients call, we never have to get him down off a mountain like with some of the young guys!"

2. *Be somewhat critical of others' evaluations.* This does not contradict the previous suggestion! How do you *really* feel about comments like "Dr. Y is marvelous. I let him make all my medical decisions," or "No. I didn't ask about side effects of that drug. I wouldn't understand it, anyway"?

3. If you are high risk, *locate a doctor used to complications.* As Dr. Karlis Adamsons, Mt. Sinai Hospital, New York City, says, "A doctor who delivers 200 babies

a year has only about 5 percent complicated cases or 10 percent. That's not much of an experience, whereas if a doctor is in charge of the complicated pregnancy clinic of a university hospital, or any hospital delivering 2,000 to 10,000 patients annually, he develops a totally different degree of expertise."

4. *Don't choose the busiest doctor in town.* He may be booked until 1984, but this very popularity means that he may spend little actual time with you. How will you feel when you receive a $50 bill for a half-hour office visit and tests, 16 minutes of which the doctor spent consulting on the phone with 4 other patients? Or when he leaves you undressed in the exam cubicle for unexplained half-hour periods?

5. *Choose an "askable" doctor.* This is pediatrician Lee Salk's advice—and it's wise. Tell your doctor early and plainly what you need or expect and any special services you desire such as genetic counseling, Lamaze classes, or other form of prepared birth. Negotiate with him about any items of United States routine care that may or may not be for you. Does he, for example, do routine episiotomy (cutting the perineum)? This is surgery ("a nice neat incision so you won't tear") in a delicate area from which some women heal only after weeks or months of difficulty. Does he hasten labor with drugs, then retard it, so it will happen during office hours—or outside office hours? Does he find fathers helpful during labor and delivery? Does he encourage immediate nursing by the baby?

Dr. Salk advised a group of expectant parents to ask their physicians about hospital care. Many reported that "when they inquired about their hospital stay in advance, they were accused of being overanxious, picayune, or untrusting. Some doctors do consider it an insult when any patient asks about their hospital affiliation. Nevertheless, I think you have every right in the world to ask for this information and to take the response you get into consideration when you make your choice. Any doctor who attempts to make you feel neurotic or is insulted by legitimate questions is simply not the doctor for you."

Dr. Howard Berk also emphasizes, "Choose a *learnable* doctor. Ask until you find one who is willing to take patient suggestions, investigate new techniques, include you in decision making. You need someone who treats you as a whole human being, not as a detached uterus with a fetus inside."

Neither Alice nor Joan was able to find an obstetrician with whom she could negotiate a matter vital to late pregnancy and nursing—a diet designed to help maintain energy. If you find your doctor's advice completely contrary to your nature or undermining to your confidence, for everyone's sake you should choose another doctor. Just say you want to seek another opinion or that you believe you will feel physically better with another kind of treatment.

Is the doctor in group practice? If so, have you met his partners? One of them may be attending you for the finale.

Dr. Berk, who has two partners, comments, "A woman comes to all three of us, but if she is my patient, I say, 'I'll handle 75 percent of your care. The other doctors will do the rest, and each will examine you on one of your next visits. With three of us, you can be sure office hours are never canceled and that you'll be attended by one of us throughout labor, not just the last five minutes because we are finishing up work here at the office.' . . .

"The role of the obstetrician should be *preventive* medicine, stopping emergencies before they occur. Emotions, for example, are the biggest part of routine obstetric care, letting people talk out their fears and worries during office visits."

In judging the doctor's approach, be alert to signs that he minimizes or maximizes problems presented to him. It's best if he does neither. Minimizing: He uses words like "simple," "just," "only." "It's simple surgery. Don't worry about it—you'll be out of the hospital the next day." Neither surgery nor anesthesia is totally without risk. "Episiotomy is just a nice, neat incision." Maximizing: Watch words like "never," "all," "dangerous," "destroyed." "A woman in your condition should *never* . . ." "Some women throw up *all* during pregnancy." "Your thyroid cells are being destroyed right now." Melodrama is fine on the stage; in pregnancy common sense and moderation are preferable.

6. Reread your health insurance booklet or policy. *Discover which services, tests, and costs are covered, which are not,* and how the coverage forms operate. As an older couple, you are apt to need more, rather than fewer, of these items. (See Chapter 17.)

After the birth of their first baby, Joan and Jay found Blue Cross coverage so inadequate that they switched to a whole new plan for covering expenses before their second baby arrived.

GYNECOLOGY EXAMINATION

Here are the components of a good exam:

1. Patient's history, including current illnesses or drugs being taken.

2. Blood pressure, urine check. The first visit should also include checking your abdomen, listening to your chest and heart. If a heart or chest problem is indicated, your obstetrician will recommend consultation with another doctor.

3. Pelvic exam—external genitals, vagina, cervix.

4. Pap smear—cells from cervix and os (mouth of cervix); checking for evidence of venereal disease.

5. Palpation of uterus.

6. Rectal exam.

7. Breast exam.

8. Psychological attitude. No gynecologist can be expected to be a psychiatrist, marriage counselor, dietitian, and sex therapist combined. All gynecologists, however, must have some training or ability in these areas. He should find out if you're depressed, overcome by anxiety, insomnia, or other mind-body interactions, and you should answer such questions honestly.

Finally, many people expect pregnant women—and new fathers—to act irrational, frantic, forgetful, craving of odd foods, etc. These are stereotypes that don't fit all women or men, but take advantage of them if you need a little extra sympathy to help you survive an otherwise blue day. If you're pregnant, let people help you into comfortable chairs, onto buses, out of cars. It may make *them* feel good!

CHAPTER 4

Genetics for the Older Couple: Roses and Thorns

"Good medicine is common sense applied to a specialized field."

Erna Wright, British childbirth educator

IF THIS OPINION IS TRUE FOR THE FINALE, birth, it is also true for management of pregnancy preceding birth. Human genetics and genetic counseling involve common sense applied to continuing the human race.

Geneticists working in cytology (the study of cell life and formation) have acquired a reputation for "test tube babies," "gene transplants," and "genetic engineering," some of which remains science fiction. In reality, genetic counselors are not attempting to construct a *Brave New World* of preprogrammed people. Their present aim is to prevent disease by detecting patients with various inherited disorders.

For some of these disorders, such as Down's syndrome (mongolism) or spina bifida (a defect in the development of the neural tube), a recent laboratory technique called amniocentesis can spot affected fetuses. Amniocentesis involves obtaining a sample of amniotic fluid (clear liquid protecting the baby within the uterus), culturing and analyzing its cells, and assaying of the fluid's components. For other disorders, like sickle cell anemia (a blood disease), Tay-Sachs (a fatal, crippling disorder), or hemophilia, one or both parents who may be carriers can now be identified through various blood tests.

One mother I met said, "My part of the Midwest has so many large families, so many menopause babies that are mongoloid. And my sister lost 8 pregnancies with the Rh factor. Neither my husband nor I wanted to be parents of a mongoloid child." This woman married at 39, had her first child at 41. "If people are going to marry older and still be parents, I think amniocentesis should be their right."

Her husband Jim added, "We didn't even tell anybody that Marg was pregnant until after amniocentesis and chromosome study had shown our baby was free of mongolism."

"Mongolism is especially heartbreaking for an older woman because she may not be able to have more children. A younger woman can try again" was the opinion of Mrs. F., an older mother of five who wanted amniocentesis during her last pregnancy because a previous baby girl had died at birth of semiunknown causes.

While some older people have the resources to be parents of two or more young children, many who marry in their thirties for a first or second time will have energy or health adequate to the challenge of only one new baby. They are wise, therefore, to do whatever possible to assure the normalcy of that one child.

Genetic counseling remains controversial, an extension of medical science's power to find and treat disease. Some couples, pregnant with a first or later child, would say, "None of those awful diseases has ever happened in our family, so why worry about it? We'll take our chances."

Ninety-five percent of prenatal diagnostic studies now done *do* demonstrate a normal fetus—for those defects tested. Biology is in some ways provident of life on this earth. However, for the 5 percent of fetuses destined to be retarded or fatally abnormal—and the thousands of parents who are not tested and could or should be—life seems unbearably wasteful of human potential.

Biologist Joshua Lederberg has estimated that one-quarter of hospital beds for the handicapped in this country are occupied by people suffering genetic diseases. Congenital and hereditary disorders are the second major cause of death of children under 5.

Dr. Kurt Hirschhorn, professor of pediatrics at Mt. Sinai Medical School, New York City, and past president of the American Society of Human Genetics, says, "Five percent of all Americans (some 10 million people) need and could profit from genetic counseling." Dr. Hirschhorn told me that Mt. Sinai was "one of the first labs in the U.S. to do prenatal diagnosis of chromosomal and biochemical defects. We began in 1969. We now diagnose 15 different disorders here. Last year we performed 350 amniotic taps, of which 150 were for advanced maternal age—37 or over. We've also done research on the chromosomal aspects of habitual spontaneous abortion that affects certain women." Dr. Hirschhorn heads the Division of Human Genetics at Mt. Sinai Hospital.

More than 2,000 different disorders are now known to be transmitted through union of faulty genes in either the sperm or the egg. These disorders are called *hereditary* or inborn, as distinct from *congenital*—those defects, like clubfoot, that occur "with birth" or in the womb during gestation. (See Chapter 8 on nutrition, drugs, and pregnancy.)

Genes are the physical and biochemical "blueprints" that direct orderly transmission of traits in all living creatures and control production and release of enzymes for proper cell, organ, and body functioning. Even sensitivity, or lack of it, to certain chemicals or drugs is now thought to be controlled by heredity.

Each human being inherits an estimated total of 200,-000 genes, arranged in precise order in double strands to form chromosomes. The healthy human being has 46 chromosomes in the nucleus of each cell, except for his or her sperm or egg cells. These sex cells each possess only 23—the full 46 when united into 23 pairs in the fertilized egg at conception of a child.

Although ancient sages speculated on how two brown-eyed parents could produce a blue-eyed baby without either a miracle or adultery, the scientific study of genetics did not begin until about 1850 with the work of the Austrian monk Johann Gregor Mendel. During the time he was studying to qualify himself to teach natural science in secondary school, he grew and observed peas in the monastery garden, noting their long or short stalks, white or red blossoms, and other characteristics.

Why peas? Availability and speed—each generation of pea plants matures in only a few weeks, and each normal cell has only 14 chromosomes. As with fruit flies, which have only 6 to 12 chromosomes, depending on species, what can be inherited is limited enough to be controllable by the researcher.

Despite work by other experimenters and theoreticians, including Charles Darwin, Mendel's discoveries lay neglected for many years. Not until 1956 did scientists agree on 46, not 48, as the correct number of human chromosomes. In 1952 British obstetrician Dr. Douglas Bevis (attacked during 1974 for embryo transplant work) had pioneered amniocentesis for checking on the severity of blood destruction suffered by an Rh baby. In this country Dr. Carlo Valenti, Downstate Medical Center, Brooklyn, used the procedure to test for the enzyme deficiency that causes Tay-Sachs disease. By 1965, amniocentesis provided fluid and cells for the first successful attempt to determine a fetal karyotype, the display of an individual's 23 pairs of chromosomes ordered by size and other specific markings.

If you ever get a chance to peer at a magnified human cell during a museum or science show, take it. At the Division of Human Genetics, Long Island Jewish-Hillside Medical Center, I saw human chromosomes "live" for the first time. The cell nucleus I saw had been cultured, stained, and mounted on a glass slide under a powerful Zeiss microscope. A collection of tiny, horizontally striped ("banded") x-shaped bodies appeared floating in a green field. They reminded me of mating caterpillars. Next I noticed they were different sized—some pairs tiny dots, others elongated.

After viewing, lab technicians photograph, cut individual chromosomes from the resulting prints, and arrange them into the neat karyotype that you see in Figure 1. Before photographing, a number of cells from each fetus are screened for consistency (to make sure the individual is not a "mosaic" with some cells normal, others abnormal).

No one has yet seen a gene. Even at 200,000-power magnification, what you observe is the horizontal dark and light striping on the chromosome pairs. Scientists only now are concluding where on a chromosome the gene or genes that control particular traits are found. Locations of some 800 are mapped, 1,000 more guessed at. This mapping of the 23 pairs of chromosomes has been compared to "searching in a cluster of mazes for an invisible animal recognizable only by his smell"!

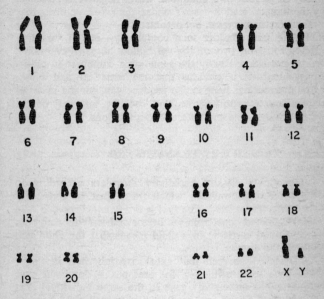

Figure 1—Normal Karyotype

All normal cells (except ova and sperm) have 46 chromosomes—44 autosomes and 2 sex chromosomes. Scientists have given these chromosomes numbers and have paired them according to their similarities. Note the sex chromosomes (XY): all normal males have one X and one Y chromosome; normal females have two X chromosomes. (These photos courtesy of Division of Human Genetics and Department of Audiovisual Resources, Long Island Jewish-Hillside Medical Center, New Hyde Park, New York 11040.)

You gaze away from the microscope awed at this spectacle of worlds within worlds, the incredible-within-the-finite—or is it, as with telescopes and outer space, the infinite? You may also newly observe the shape of your hand or the tissue of a cut finger—and wonder how your parents knew what they were doing when they assembled you. Or if your own childhood was a negative experience, you may be glad it wasn't under their full control, that they were only agents, not organizers!

When you consider such complexity—except for identical twins, no two of the 40 billion humans ever alive have possessed exactly the same gene combination or arrangement—it is obvious that mathematical and mutational errors can happen. To produce you, genetic material from your ancestors got shuffled, cardlike, into only one of 8 million possible and different combinations.

HOW TROUBLE IS TRANSMITTED

Geneticists classify hereditary disorders according to the three main ways by which traits, that is, genes, for them are transmitted. The first is *dominant:* Presence of a single affected gene from mother or father (either or both are affected carriers) in a child means that the child will inherit the disease.

Mendel discovered that genes are inherited in pairs: The gene for brown eyes, for example, is dominant over the blue-eye (recessive) gene in the same individual. Yet brown-eyed people can produce a blue-eyed child because somebody's grandma or grandpa had blue eyes, and this gene is what the child received from both mother and father. This is a familiar, and harmless, example. If, however, a defect is caused by a dominant gene, that gene will mask the effect of its normal partner, creating the disorder. Nearly 1,000 diseases, including Huntington's chorea, a degenerative neurologic disorder of middle age that killed folk singer Woody Guthrie, are transmitted in this way. Each child in the affected family has a 50 percent chance of inheriting the disease. If he is lucky, he will inherit the carrier parent's normal gene.

In a *recessive* disorder, the effect of the recessive, disease-bearing gene is hidden by the normal dominant gene for the trait. The parent, while not a victim, is a carrier. When two carriers of a recessive disorder produce a child, the baby has a one in four chance of being affected, that is, he inherits two recessive defective genes; a two in four chance of being a healthy carrier (he inherits one recessive defective gene); and a one in four chance of being neither carrier nor victim (he inherits no defective genes for this disorder). This is statistically true for *every* birth within an affected family. Because one child is already afflicted with a recessive disorder such as sickle cell anemia, Tay-Sachs, or cystic fibrosis, this fact does not mean that the disease will pass over three or four children before striking again. The odds are the same whether the child is first-born, last-born, or anywhere in between.

There are more than 800 known recessive diseases. Dr. Hirschhorn says, "Every human being carries from three to eight harmful recessive genes."

The third group is both recessive and *sex-linked:* The disease gene, as for hemophilia, appears only on the X, or female, sex chromosome. More research will probably discover diseases carried through the Y, or male, chromosome. A mother (Queen Victoria of England is the infamous example) has two female (XX) sex chromosomes. She does not suffer from hemophilia because her normal X-dominant gene masks the X-recessive disease gene. However, her sons (males are XY and lack a second normal X as protection against a defective X) have a one in two chance of inheriting the disease-bearing X; her daughters have a one in two chance of being carriers.

In Queen Victoria's case, 8 of her 25 male descendants were hemophiliacs. Her eighth child, Leopold, died at 31 from the disease. Her daughter Alice transmitted the gene to granddaughter Alix, who married the last czar of Russia before the 1917 revolution. Their fifth child, the long-awaited male heir to the Russian throne, turned out to be hemophiliac.

About 85 conditions, including baldness and color blindness, are identified as X-linked; another 65 are probable.

One-quarter million babies are born yearly in the U.S. with significant birth defects. Of these, about 20 percent are caused by heredity; 20 percent by birth environment, which includes factors such as drugs and prenatal infection; and 60 percent by some interaction between genes and environment.

CHROMOSOMAL DISORDERS—20,000
U.S. BABIES YEARLY

Another kind of genetic error occurs when one whole
chromosome (instead of a specific gene or genes) is damaged or when something goes wrong with cell division
leading to too many or too few chromosomes. Examples
of disorders resulting from 47 (one too many) chromosomes are most cases of Down's syndrome and Klinefelter's
syndrome (boys with XYY cells). A disorder from 45
(one too few) chromosomes is Turner's syndrome (girls
with only one X chromosome). This means that every cell
of the developing embryo is "miscast" with an inevitable
compounding of physical and mental abnormalities, although Down's syndrome is the most serious of these disorders.

About 65 different chromosomal or biochemical disorders can now be diagnosed via blood or cell studies. Some
tests involve detection of carrier parents; others detect affected fetuses. A few disorders, especially infant failure
to produce certain enzymes, can be treated with diet after
birth if diagnosed in time.

Common problems are:

Disorder	U.S. Group Most Affected
	(No race or group is immune.)
cystic fibrosis (lungs)	1 in 1,500 white births
	1 in 20 white adult carriers
sickle cell anemia (blood)	40,000–50,000 victims
	2.5 million black carriers
Tay-Sachs (brain, nervous system)	1 in 6,000 births of Jews with East European ancestry;
	1 in 40 such Jews a carrier
spina bifida, anencephaly (neural tube, nervous system)	Northern European, especially Irish
PKU (inability to digest protein)	Irish, other Celtic peoples 100,000 female carriers, 20,000 male child victims.
Down's syndrome (mental and physical retardation)	20-year-olds: 1 in 2,300 births 35–39-year-olds: 1 in 64 births 40–44-year-olds: 1 in 39 births

DOWN'S SYNDROME

The above figures for Down's syndrome speak for themselves, making it the disorder of prime importance to older couples considering pregnancy. Over 90 percent of present amniocentesis is performed to detect Down's syndrome.

Only in 1959 was the extra chromosome (Trisomy 21) form of Down's discovered (Fig. 2). This accounts for some 95 percent of the disease. The other 5 percent is caused by broken chromosomes (translocation). A piece of one broken chromosome may attach itself to another broken chromosome (Fig. 3).

Pediatrician Virginia Apgar estimates that mongolism costs $1.7 billion per year. Dr. René Jahiel, of the Scientists' Committee for Public Information, New York City, estimates that care for each institutionalized Down's syndrome child costs $10,000 per year and $300,000 for the average life span of 30 years, although many such children are not institutionalized unless they develop other medical problems, such as heart disease. Many parents learn to care for them at home.

In a study of 200 families with a Down's syndrome child, Dr. Murray Feingold, Professor of Pediatrics, Tufts University, Boston, reports, "There is tremendous variation of mental retardation with Down's syndrome, but it is rare to have no retardation at all. Seventy-three percent of children achieved better than parents had expected, 23 percent as expected, 4 percent worse." These parents had evidently been well counseled in what to expect.

If you were a mother pregnant with a second Down's syndrome child, would you want to know? Fifty-eight percent of women said yes, 23 percent no, 5 percent unsure, 14 percent no answer.

Would you choose to have the baby if you knew?

Thirty-two percent would have the baby; 35 percent would not—they would choose abortion; 19 percent were unsure what they would do.

Of the 35 percent choosing abortion, 65 percent were Catholic, 20 percent Protestant, 15 percent Jewish or unaffiliated. The amount of education, rather than religious preference, proved the crucial factor; the more educated

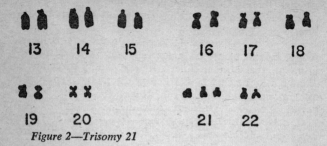

Figure 2—Trisomy 21

Trisomy 21, the chief cause of Down's syndrome, refers to a condition in which there are three, rather than the usual two, chromosomes in the 21 pair. Trisomy 21 usually results from a mistake in cell division of either the egg or the sperm and is an accidental occurrence. This photo is a simulated view of the condition. An artist has grouped and numbered photos of actual pairs of chromosomes, highly magnified, from one cell of an individual with Down's syndrome.

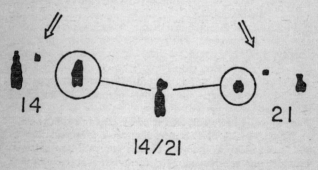

Figure 3—Formation of a Translocation Chromosome

A translocation occurs when a piece of one chromosome breaks off and attaches to a different chromosome. The translocation chromosome, the probable cause of Down's syndrome in this individual, has been formed by the breaking and rejoining of one each of the chromosome pairs 14 and 21, with loss of the little pieces (arrows). Simulated view of actual chromosomes from a human cell.

parents (those with probably more money) would risk another Down's child; less educated parents preferred abortion.

It is no doubt impossible to estimate the strains that a retarded child places on a marriage or the constant adjustments that normal children in the family must make. Although 38 percent of Dr. Feingold's couples reported a more positive marriage relationship, and 57 percent reported no change, this seems exceedingly optimistic.

One New York couple I met, already parents of a 9-year-old affected child, would not have dared pregnancy again without amniocentesis. The woman said, "If I decided to have a child knowing it was deformed, my husband would blame me for the rest of my life. I would blame myself. A second deformed child would probably cause a divorce. Amniocentesis meant a great deal to us. Yet we learned about it only by accident while at the hospital for our first child's problems."

The husband added, "I love my son, but I would have chosen abortion for a second deformed baby." The second baby proved healthy and was 4 months old at the time of the interview.

Another father, upon learning his new child was mongoloid, said, "When the doctor told me, I went home and just cried."

Why do these genetic problems occur? Why are older women especially susceptible? (Of course, individual older men with genes for a dominant disorder or with otherwise defective sperm cells can produce mutations which cause abnormalities, too.)

At the present time the catalyst for Down's syndrome—an extra chromosome occurring before or immediately after fertilization—is known. However, even this catalyst, which seems specific enough, remains a cause without a reason. A woman is born with some 2 million immature eggs, produced when her ovaries were formed (in the seventh month of gestation). This incredible number probably results from combining powerful maternal estrogens with the hormones also being produced by the female fetus as it develops. At adolescence perhaps one-half million eggs are left, and only a mere 400 are used in an average lifetime of menstrual cycles. By the time a woman is 35, her eggs are also 35+ years old. Her fertility depends not on cells produced like sperm every few days or months but on maturing of eggs created before her own birth. Her body has also absorbed nearly four decades of x-rays, ultraviolet light, drugs, chemicals, drink, food, which may all hurt the delicate egg.

In 1970 a Paris geneticist, Jerome LeJeune, announced a study correlating 12 Down's syndrome babies with intercourse that had happened early in their mothers' menstrual cycles (7 to 10 days). He concluded that the ovaries of these women tend to release eggs before they are fully mature, "before all enzymes responsible for orderly meiosis have been produced" (*Medical World News,* January 16, 1970).

Another theory is that eggs fertilized when "overripe" (too many hours after release from the ovary) also produce defective embryos.

Dr. Hirschhorn comments, "With all these theories—overripe eggs, aging ovary, reduced intercourse in older couples—there remains a statistical limit. No one explanation can yet account for the combined incidence of mongolism." He adds, *"All* chromosome disorders, not just Down's syndrome, are maternal age-related."

It is useful to remember one other fact about the incidence of Down's syndrome. While older women are at greater risk, that is, produce a greater *percentage* of mongoloid babies per number of normal births compared with younger mothers, it is women under 35 who still produce the greater *absolute number* of these children.

Before the extra chromosome was understood, researchers found other interesting material. Fluoride in drinking water has been blamed—and praised—as many things, including a Communist conspiracy. European women now take fluor tablets to prevent tooth decay with no apparent ill effects, especially if they are young. But studies made from 1950 to 1956 by Dr. Lionel Rapaport, then of the Psychiatric Institute, University of Wisconsin, which examined the incidence of mongoloid births in four states—Wisconsin, Illinois, North and South Dakota—indicated that there is a definite relationship between the concentration of fluoride in the drinking water and the frequency of mongolism.

He became interested in the problem of fluorides when he noticed, in studying mongolism, that such children have very little tooth decay compared to normal children who eat the same diet. He also discovered from the work of other researchers that oxygen consumption in the brains of mongoloid children is lowered, resulting in their characteristic brain deficiency. This indicates incomplete development of the enzymatic equipment of the brain. Fluorine has a definite effect on certain enzymes. It is an "inhibitor"—that is, it stops their activity. And some enzymes present in brain tissues are fluoride sensitive.

He presented his research in *The Bulletin of the National Academy of Medicine* in France (140, 1956; 143, 1959). Here are his figures for the state of Illinois:

In towns where the fluoride content is 0.0 to 0.2 milligrams per liter of water, there are 34.15 cases of mongolism per 100,000 births [1 per 2,928], whereas in towns where there are 0.3 to 0.7 milligrams of fluorine per liter of water, there are 47.07 cases of mongolism per 100,000; and finally where there are 1.0 to 2.6 milligrams of fluorine per liter of water, there are as many as 71.59 cases of mongolism per 100,000 births [1 per 1,397].

Other interesting facts: The average age of Down's syndrome mothers in high fluorine areas was *lower* than normal. There were twice as many affected babies at 2.6 mg. per liter (2.6 parts per million) as at 0.2. Critics attacked this work by saying that as long as figures do not begin to approach the 1 per 39 births figure for women above 40, for example, then no one should be alarmed.

In 1966 the FDA did ban use of fluorine in prenatal drugs, although it is still present in drinking water and most toothpaste.

The following is a thought-provoking case treated by Dr. Anna Szasz of Budapest, Hungary. It was reported in an article in the German medical journal, *Monatschrift fur Kinderheitkunde* (1949), and discusses effects of vitamins A and E on maternal and fetal metabolism, blood circulation, and glands.

Dr. Szasz describes a middle-aged couple—the husband was epileptic, the mother anemic with low basal metabolism. Within five years, four daughters were born to the couple. The first three were all mongoloid, each one more afflicted than the last. At the fourth pregnancy Dr. Szasz tried to improve the mother's health by giving her glanduantin (hormone extract), thyroid extract, liver, iron, and all the vitamins, including plentiful dosage of E. The mother was sent to a mountain resort, rested a good deal, ate a high-protein diet plus plenty of liver and vegetables. The baby was born at the proper time—completely normal and healthy.

This may be a medical miracle, but it seems only common sense that a mother's body cannot furnish a developing fetus with the proper nutrients if she doesn't possess them herself. The fetus will "take what it needs"—an obstetric slogan of the Forties and Fifties—only if the mother has supplies to share.

Hepatitis infection and work with radar equipment have also been listed as possible causes of Down's syndrome.

One man I met, a World War II radar technician, later fathered two sons, both mentally retarded with multiple problems involving speech and muscular coordination. The wife had wanted more children but didn't dare try again.

THE COUNSELING PROCESS

Suppose you and your husband are 35 or older and want to guarantee that the child you plan or are already carrying will not be afflicted with Down's syndrome or other disorder. During pregnancy, where do you go? Whom do you consult?

Upon confirmation of pregnancy, consult with the doctor who takes your family and personal medical history. Ask about amniocentesis for Down's syndrome or other disorders for which you may be at risk. If the doctor is your obstetrician, he may be trained in the amniocentesis procedure. It may be done in his office or, more probably, at a clinic or medical center during your fourth month of pregnancy (15 to 17 weeks after your last menstrual period).

Possibly he may declare, as did two obstetricians I interviewed, "The fetus has a privacy which shouldn't be invaded" or "95 percent of babies are normal. Why bother?"

If you get no cooperation and remain worried, consult

a book called *International Directory of Genetic Services*, published by National Foundation-March of Dimes and available in the reference section of many large libraries. The 1974 directory listed 890 scientists and centers for human genetics in which counseling may be obtained; 251 of these centers offer amniocentesis. Write or phone and ask to speak with a physician or genetic counselor in the laboratory or division of human genetics. It is crucial to lose no time because amniocentesis for Down's syndrome can be done only in midpregnancy—not before you are pregnant or after delivery. Before you become pregnant, you and your husband can be tested, on the basis of your age and history, for other disorders for which prenatal diagnosis may be available.

Prenatal diagnosis allows the doctor, for the first time in human history, to state unequivocally that certain defects are or are not present. Provided the test is properly done, you receive actual information about the fetus, rather than a general calculation of probability about its condition based on no direct evidence.

To discover what happens at a human genetics center, I visited Dr. Ernest Lieber, a geneticist, and his assistant, Mrs. Audrey Heimler, a genetic counselor. They work at the Division of Human Genetics, Long Island Jewish-Hillside Medical Center in New Hyde Park, New York, on Long Island's north shore. The procedures I describe are standard in most genetic units.

Besides following up tests and counseling current patients, Dr. Lieber and Mrs. Heimler work with several new individuals or couples per week. Dr. Lieber is an internist who has specialized in human genetics. When I expressed surprise that he isn't a gynecologist, he reminded me that genetics intersects so many medical disciplines—neurology, hematology, skeletal defects, heart and vascular diseases, etc.—that it attracts a most varied research group. He has a genuine interest in people and their problems.

I asked him about genetic engineering, a futuristic field that has achieved some success at injecting enzymes into an individual who lacks a functioning gene for the enzyme —and may eventually transplant whole genes, construct an artificial womb, even a "cloned" baby with only one parent.

He answered, "Of course, these things are discussed but

are of little importance at our daily work level." About drugs he admits honestly, "Thalidomide caused certain, unmistakable damage in about 20 percent of those mothers and fetuses exposed. For most drugs, however, we just don't know yet. Not enough work has been completed."

Most mothers or couples consult Dr. Lieber or Mrs. Heimler after birth of an affected child. A pediatrician or neurologist, sometimes one affiliated with the medical center, has diagnosed the baby's abnormalities. Parents want to know why—as well as the chance of a recurrence with another birth.

Interviews begin in Mrs. Heimler's office. A graduate (M.S.) of Sarah Lawrence College's new program in genetics and counseling techniques, she also received a B.A. in psychology. Her office wall displays an appropriate photo poster that reads, "We can complain because rose bushes have thorns or rejoice because thorn bushes have roses."

During a first interview she tries to put a couple at ease while determining as much as possible about their family histories and the nature of the problem. Many patients are examined by doctors in the genetics unit for medical conditions.

Suppose you are consulting a physician and the counselor who works with him or her at a genetic unit. It is your first pregnancy. Since there is no history of genetic defect in your family, you have every reason to hope your baby will be healthy—but you want to make sure, especially concerning Down's syndrome. If you live near a center and are not yet 15 to 17 weeks pregnant, a physician or counselor will take your history and determine whether there is a risk in your case for Down's syndrome or other genetic disorders. If prenatal diagnosis is indicated, you will receive an appointment on a future date for actual amniocentesis. With pictures and diagrams, she or he will explain how it is done, what is being tested for, and the minor risks of the test itself. She or he will give you an informed consent paper to read and consider.

If there's no reason to rush, the counselor tries not to schedule amniocentesis for your first appointment. Couples need time to think, discuss, prepare emotionally. You are offered the test whatever your views on abortion. A Roman Catholic couple, for instance, need not fear that, should deformity be diagnosed, they will be relentlessly pressured into aborting the fetus. It is understood that a small percentage of couples may want prenatal diagnosis for their own information or to provide early treatment for a newborn but would not want to terminate the pregnancy.

At Long Island Jewish and other institutions, amniocentesis is performed when there is an increased risk of a chromosome disorder such as Down's syndrome; for spina bifida and anencephaly (neurologic disorders of the spine or brain) detected by elevated levels of alpha-fetoprotein in the amniotic fluid; for certain metabolic disorders, such as Tay-Sachs disease; and for sex determination (males) when there is a risk for a sex-linked disorder such as hemophilia or Duchenne's muscular dystrophy.

On the appointed day you appear for the test. What happens first is a painless scan (sonography) of your abdomen with a sound-wave machine. A long metal arm with sensitive head glides over you and obtains a sonogram—a rough picture that allows the gynecologist who will perform the fluid "tap" to measure the baby's head, size of uterus, location of placenta, and whether you are carrying more than one child. Sonography was developed by the U.S. Navy for underwater research.

The doctor re-examines your abdomen, prepares a spot on the abdominal wall, injects local anesthesia, and inserts a long needle, mounted with syringe, through abdominal and uterine walls until he senses fluid. He avoids both baby and placenta. In a thin woman he need not insert deeply. When the plunger top is retracted, fluid rises into the syringe. He hopes to obtain 10 to 15 cc.—about 1 ounce. He carefully closes the vial, labels it, and sends or delivers it to the laboratory.

All this sounds formidable but can be done in a few minutes as an outpatient procedure. It's a kind of reverse injection. I heard several reactions from older women about the procedure. They seemed as varied as the women. When one was advised to "take the rest of the day off," she asked, "Why? I feel fine." She returned immediately to her store to sort merchandise.

Another reported, "The doctor had to insert the needle twice because he failed to get fluid the first time. The second time I felt intense pressure, but the clear fluid came out." A third, mother of a previous child who had died at birth, said, "I did feel the tap and was uncomfortable for three days. I felt the puncture of the needle as discomfort and was quite nauseous afterward, unusual for me. Some of it may have been mental. I had to take a long car trip the next day."

In the laboratory the fluid is centrifuged; a round, brown machine about a foot high whirls it at elevated speed to settle the cells into a white mass under the clear yellow liquid. Then the cells are cultured in an incubator for 2 1/2 to 5 weeks. Dr. Lieber told me 19 days is average in his laboratory.

Why so long? The cells must grow and reproduce. Outside the uterus this is no more instant a process than within the developing child.

Occasionally cells fail to grow; a second tap is needed to obtain more fluid. After adequate growth, cells are washed in special solution to "fix" them and swell the chromosomes for easier viewing. Under the microscope a technician samples a number of cells for uniformity. Chromosomes in some of the cells are photographed, the photos enlarged, and the karyotype prepared. Dr. Lieber examines results, then notifies the couple's doctor of the presumably good news—the child is free of those defects tested for.

One woman said, "I hadn't told anybody I was pregnant, and I had anxiety dreams while awaiting the amniocentesis results. Then my doctor called me at 10 o'clock on a Friday night with the good news. He said he didn't want me to have to wait until Monday. That was so nice of him."

The child's sex is also evident from the arranged set of chromosomes if the parents desire to know it. Most do, although some don't ask. The whole procedure, including tap, ultrasound, chromosome study, counseling, and record keeping, currently costs about $200 plus obstetrician's fee for the tap.

Amniocentesis requires further study and research. It is not without minor flaws. All equipment must be sterile; the obstetrician must try to avoid mixing blood with the amniotic fluid. The fluid sample is then sent to the laboratory, which may be in the same building or across a city. Dr. Aubrey Milunsky of Harvard Medical School and Massachusetts General Hospital, who has coordinated a 9-center U.S. study of amniocentesis, reported he has received usable fluid flown all the way from South Africa.

Here are results of a 1971 study of amniocentesis by Dr. Henry Nadler of Chicago: Of 1,000 women receiving amniocentesis, no maternal death or fetal malformation resulted. A few cases of spontaneous abortion occurred one to three months afterward. Risk to the mother was less than 1 in 1,000; risk to the fetus, less than 1 in 500. Dr. Hirschhorn calls it "a low-risk procedure" when properly done.

Results of a 4-year, 9-center study were announced in late 1975; 1,040 pregnant women in the U.S. who received amniocentesis were compared with 992 who did not. In the first group, 34 abnormal fetuses were diagnosed. An additional 11 mothers were found to be carrying male fetuses, each having a 50 percent risk of a sex-linked disorder such as hemophilia or muscular dystrophy; 35 of these 45 women chose therapeutic abortion. Of the 992 who did not receive amniocentesis, 7 bore Down's syndrome babies.

For both groups, the rate of fetal loss (from miscarriage and stillbirth) was similar—3.5 percent of women who had amniocentesis versus 3.2 percent of those who did not.

GENETIC COUNSELING AND YOUR EMOTIONS

Unlike a urine or Pap test, amniocentesis takes time—usually a month. After sonography had determined the size of the fetal head, one woman turned out to be four more weeks pregnant than everybody had thought. Had she needed and agreed to abortion, she might have just missed the legal limit of 24 weeks in New York State.

How do couples feel about the whole process?

Many are grateful that it makes the final months of pregnancy relatively worry free, although waiting for the cell culture results can be anxious. Some couples, already parents of an afflicted child, wouldn't dare pregnancy again without amniocentesis.

And what, exactly, do they learn through it?

Before you decide for or against genetic counseling, consider the following study of it as an educational experiment. Evaluate the results, which are curious.

The title is "Genetic Counseling: A Consumer's View." It appeared in *New England Journal of Medicine* (287:

433–39, 1972). Counseling occurred at Johns Hopkins Hospital, Baltimore, during 1969–70, was evaluated by Dr. Claire Leonard and others, and included families of children afflicted with cystic fibrosis or Down's syndrome or phenylketonuria (PKU), plus a control group of children with juvenile arthritis.

The parents of these 61 families with genetic disorders were educated to varying degrees by physicians, professional counseling, participation in Cystic Fibrosis Foundation work, receiving its literature, etc.

Did all this succeed?

Five families claimed never to have been counseled at all. . . . Parents of five other families observed said that the genetic information given at the time of diagnosis or shortly thereafter was not retained because of emotional shock.

Four families who acknowledged that they had been counseled claimed inability to understand genetics, and five others were unable to apply their knowledge of probability and the genetic risks to their specific case. This group included a mother who understood that the risks were statistical and who thus concluded that unless she was planning to have a family of hundreds, the genetic risk figures were of no relevance to her. . . ,

In six families the element of denial was so strong that the parents could not accept some aspects of the counseling. One mother believed that her severely affected child with cystic fibrosis had a good prognosis; another refused to have the siblings tested, and a third stated that the disease was nongenetic. One father, unable to accept that he could carry a gene for an illness, denied paternity. . . .

Parental knowledge of the genetics of their children's diseases was significantly related to their educational level, their comprehension of probabilities, their general biological knowledge, and whether or not they had heard of the disease before experiencing it. . . .

Repression, denial, guilt, misunderstanding, these are very human reactions to situations that were no doubt filled with the tension, anguish, and crisis that illness brings. These families couldn't and didn't enjoy the "luxury" of prenatal diagnosis or amniocentesis. They were coping with the dietary, behavioral, and developmental problems of already afflicted children.

It is also natural for the doctors and counselors to wonder why their best efforts at education seemed ineffective for about one-quarter of the families studied. As with most interactions, faults on both sides probably combined to produce some failure.

The very newness of genetic counseling is not the least of reasons for apprehension, misapprehension, and controversy. When gynecology itself became a specialty in the nineteenth century, Victorian morality encouraged many woman to avoid treatment for diseases of the reproductive organs—and many men to avoid diagnosis of venereal disease.

Today a woman or couple may still maintain they'd rather not know, but the routineness and wide knowledge of Pap tests and breast-screening procedures have at least removed the horror and shame. As genetic counseling grows in acceptance and availability, couples will ideally consider it an aid to family planning and health care—not, as with mental illness, a fearful admission of failure.

"A DEMONSTRATION PROJECT FOR THE U.S."

In New York City the Scientists' Committee for Public Information (SCPI), led by Dr. René Jahiel, is proposing an impressive program of genetic counseling and amniocentesis for women over 35. For months Dr. Jahiel has met and planned with groups of genetic counselors, public health scientists, older parents, obstetricians, laboratory directors.

From a present annual total of 500 women receiving amniocentesis in New York City—less than 7 percent of the pregnant New York population over 35—the new services would expand to reach a potential 7,000 pregnant women yearly. Those over 35 are of special concern, but the program aims to include those of any age who already have a child with either Down's syndrome or neural tube defect (because of significant recurrence risk and statistics) or those who themselves carry sex-linked diseases. Besides chromosome disorders and neural tube defects, the New York program will identify pregnant couples whose history indicates risk of biochemical abnormalities, such as Tay-Sachs or galactosemia (inability to digest milk products), and refer them to another laboratory for study.

The SCPI task force is setting guidelines to reach parents, arrange appropriate tests in approved facilities, hire trained personnel, keep records, evaluate results. Funding will come from several sources, including government, health insurance, and patient fees on a sliding scale. Television, videotape, newspaper and pamphlet announcements of the program are planned.

This would be the first prenatal diagnostic program of such magnitude in the U.S. As genetic counselor Audrey Heimler said at a hospital meeting, "Genetic counseling is preventive medicine. We are motivating people to seek information and testing." In its potential for public education and aiding couples to achieve more worry-free pregnancy, this project should serve, according to Dr. Jahiel, as "a demonstration project for the rest of the country. Women will be eligible for amniocentesis whether they intend or do not intend to have abortion if abnormality is found."

Counselors would offer advice and arrangements if abortion is desired. In Dr. Aubrey Milunsky's words, however: "The decision to procreate or abort a pregnancy is a parental right which must not be superseded by any directive from the physician, acting in accord with his own, or worse, with society's religious, eugenic, or other dictates." He adds, "Despite all compelling efforts by patients to have their physician make decisions for them, it seems wiser to resist such appeals."

Doctors and counselors are, of course, legally and ethically at risk if they either force a patient into an action or withhold information on which a decision can be based. A counselor told me that a "majority" of her patients carrying proven abnormal babies do choose abortion— but some do not. Even after birth of a normal child, some amniocentesis parents admit, "We still don't know what we would have decided if we'd been told our baby was abnormal."

The New York City program would also serve pregnant couples from the suburbs or elsewhere. No woman at risk would be turned away without advice or help.

Amniocentesis and genetic counseling programs are

already well functioning in New York despite the city's well-publicized medical insurance and financial crises. The challenge and goal will be to extend these programs to serve as many people with varying health needs as possible.

CHAPTER 5

Multiple Births:
What Are Your Chances?

SOMEBODY ONCE DEFINED TWINS AS "WHEN you wish there were two of them but four of you."

One of my respondents, a teacher named Nusia who lives on a farm in French Canada, gave birth to unexpected twins, a boy and a girl, when she was about 35 and her husband 40. "In my case, my parents had just about given up hope that I'd ever get married and have children. My husband and I decided it was time to start a family and were glad we were able to.

"The birth of the twins didn't change our *ideas* on the place of children in our lives, but physically we just existed *around* their schedule of feedings. With two, each on a different timetable, there wasn't much time for sleep in between. Since my husband shared in the work, both of us were exhausted."

To my question "What is the most important thing you're learning through being a parent?" she answered, "Honesty. You have to do and live what you say to your children. Also, I like having children better than not having any."

When I last saw her, she was musing on why her boy

and girl, exactly the same age, raised by the same parents, were acquiring such different personalities. Was it the sex difference? Or different genes—since her children are fraternal, not identical, twins?

An honorable parental question. To date, psychologists have no definitive explanation for sibling differences. Adam and Eve probably wondered about Cain and Abel. No doubt Rebecca and Isaac, 40 when he married and 60 at fatherhood, also had questions about their twins, Jacob and Esau, who followed Cain and Abel in differing on the merits of hunting versus farming or sheep herding, among other things. So much did the twins "jostle each other within her" that Rebecca, who had previously worried about infertility, was driven to ask, "Why am I pregnant?"

HOW TWINS HAPPEN

Twins—both identical (monozygotic, from one fertilized egg) and fraternal (dizygotic, from two eggs)—occur naturally in one of every 86 births throughout the world.

This is a statistical average determined by combining the rate for identical twins (3.5 sets per 1,000 births, constant for all races) with the rate for fraternal twins, which varies by race. Whites produce fraternal twins on an average of one set per 105 births (8 sets per 1,000). For Oriental peoples, it is one set per 460 births (2.5 per 1,000). Blacks average six times this—one set per 70 to 75 births. The Yoruba of Africa are the world's champion twinners—40 to 42 sets per 1,000 births.

Age at marriage, birth control, nutrition, and desired family size obviously influence these rates, but the prime reason for the differences is not sociologic but biologic. Human beings are mammals, and the genetic rule decrees that *within* a species (homo sapiens) the race largest in body size produces the largest litter size. This is sound sense for assuring survival of individuals. Blacks of certain African tribes are tall, stately people; whites are average, while an Oriental woman, who may weigh less than 90 pounds, cannot easily produce twins or triplets of adequate survival size.

The above data by race are averaged to include all childbearing ages. There are exceptions—"super statistics"

—and it is older couples who produce them. Couples over 35 have identical twins at 4 sets per 1,000 births, compared with 3.5 for women under 25. The fraternal twinning rate rises gradually through a woman's twenties, maximizes when she is 35 to 40, then declines. It peaks at age 37. A white woman of less than 20 has the least chance of bearing twins, 6.4 sets per 1,000 live births. A woman of 37 who has already borne several children has a much greater chance, 16.8 sets per 1,000 live births, which is double the average for whites. And a woman of any age who is already the mother of fraternal twins has about four times the chance of bearing a second set, compared with other women in her age group.

Fraternal twinning peaks at 37 because the female secretion of gonadotropin hormone from the pituitary gland, which controls the timing and release of the monthly egg(s), maximizes at this age. Twinning also runs in families; generations of daughters possibly inherit the gene or genes stimulating gonadotropin production.

As with any biologic process, irregularities can occur. The early months of marriage produce more twins; for first births the rate is 9.8 sets per 1,000. More frequent intercourse probably stimulates what is called "double ovulation" or "superfecundation." Two eggs, produced, fertilized, and implanted separately, create fraternal twins. Such babies need not even have the same father! In 1947 a married woman delivered male and female twins. Blood tests of both revealed that the husband fathered the boy, and another man fathered the girl. An 1810 report tells of a white woman who had intercourse with a white man and a black man within a few days. Nine months later she delivered one white and one mulatto twin.

Rates for natural tripletting, quadrupletting, etc., also maximize at maternal age 35 to 40. They follow the same ratio as for twinning. Triplets are 86 times as rare (1 in 7,396 births) as twins; quads 86 times rarer than triplets (1 in 636,056 births).

Twins, triplets, etc., can originate from the division of one egg after fertilization into halves, thirds, or fourths, or from some combination of multiple eggs that are fertilized separately. Some then subdivide into new embryos; one or two may continue growth without creating more embryos. The Dionne quints, born in 1935, were from one egg. The Diligenti quints, born in Argentina in 1943, were probably from three eggs. If one fertilized egg can produce triplets, two eggs may also. Obstetricians classify these births according to whether the babies share one amniotic sac and one divided umbilical cord or each baby has one of each item. Other possibilities are one sac, two cords or one divided cord, two sacs. This matters not for mathematics but for fetal nutrition and development.

Beyond race, it is not known what effect the father or his age plays in multiple births. Studies are contradictory so far. Effect of father's age "is small if it exists at all," according to one expert, Dr. M. G. Bulmer.

Basically, multiple births seem to be determined by the mother, her age, genes, monthly number and condition of her egg cells. If this sounds similar to the situation that produces chromosomal abnormalities, such as Down's syndrome, it is unfortunately so. Geneticists, obstetricians, and pediatricians consider multiple births as high-risk events because these pregnancies from inception are contests for survival of the fittest.

Multiple births are difficult because rates for complications soar. Maternal toxemia (failure of the uterine blood supply to meet fetal demand), which occurs in 5 to 10 percent of single pregnancies, triples for twins. Malpresentation at birth, which leads to long labor, has these rates:

	Single Birth (percent)	Twins (percent)
Vertex (normal; head down)	95	63
Breech (feet first)	3	30
Transverse (baby horizontal)	.5	4.5
Other	1.5	2.5

Frequency of congenital malformations doubles for identical twins, compared with single births; 50 percent of twins are born prematurely by several weeks, compared with 8 percent of single births. The reason seems to be physical or mechanical: To safeguard maternal health and life, the pregnant uterus begins contractions when it surpasses a weight of about 12 pounds. Twins, although individually small, together reach this weight on an average three weeks earlier than the usual full term of nine months. Statistics reflect this. Average birth weight for "singletons" is 7 pounds; twins, 5 pounds each; triplets, 4 pounds each; quadruplets, 3 pounds. The stillbirth rate shows a similar progression: For twins it doubles; triplet triple it; quadruplets quadruple it. Neonatal (first month) death rate for twins is 5 times that for single births; for triplets, it is 20 times. During the first and second years these elevated rates become lower and eventually are no different from rates for single births. That is, healthy 2-year-old twins are no more subject to medical emergencies than other toddlers.

For birth defects, such as cerebral palsy or mental retardation, twins test at rates similar to other premature babies. One study (Drillien, 1968) found that at seven years of age about 20 percent of children with birth weights of 3 1/2 to 4 1/2 pounds were "moderately to severely handicapped," as were over 50 percent of children who weighed less than 3 1/4 pounds at birth.

Another study found twins "less intelligent by an average of 5 I.Q. points" than single-birth children. Because I.Q. testing is now in a period of re-evaluation, this figure is not of such crucial range or importance compared with statistics for toxemia or malpresentation. However, it does reinforce the general impression: Multiple births are purposely rare because they have low survival potential for the individual and species. This is natural eugenics at work.

Of fraternal boy-girl twins, the female babies, who mature faster before and after birth than boys, generally do better. This is the start of the life differential between the sexes. Women, though smaller and weaker in physical stature and strength, live longer than men.

Throughout human history, people have celebrated the occurrence of twins with literature and legend. In the last hundred years scientists and psychologists have found in identical twins a nearly perfect human genetic laboratory since they share the same sex and genetic programming.

Identical, and sometimes fraternal, twins resemble each other more than they resemble other siblings in a family. This remains true even for identical twins raised apart because of war, family or other social problems. Some of this can be ascribed to optical illusion and suggestibility. Because people encourage twins to dress and act alike, they do what is expected—respond alike.

This does not preclude, however, playing games of retribution on parents, baby sitters, or each other. Twin sisters Judy and Jill, adults with (twin) Ph.D.s in psychology, once told me about their adolescence. Since they regularly failed to get people to treat them as individuals, Jill, who was always less popular than Judy, devised some teen-age vengeance. Judy had accepted a prom date with Danny, "the class drag." Then the class hero phoned her for the same prom. She accepted him, also. After Jill had gotten no date, Judy talked her into dating unpopular Danny and pretending Jill was Judy for the evening. In the gym, full of dim lights and girls who had left their glasses home, nobody—not even the boys—noticed there were two Judys and apparently no Jill.

Judy arrived home triumphant, Jill quiet after her incognito evening with Danny. Finally, Judy noticed something different about her sister and asked, "What's that class ring around your neck?"

"Oh, it's Danny's," Jill replied. "Tonight *Judy* accepted him. And you're going steady with him from now on."

Scientific studies of twinning began in this century. For historical work, a genetic researcher needs a stable, homogeneous, literate population that values accurate family record keeping. Not many countries or groups in the world qualify. The U.S., for instance, has been slandered as "a geneticist's nightmare." Twinning researchers have worked in Sweden, England, Iceland, Germany (Stuttgart has records from 1790–1900, published in 1909), and in this country with Mormon Church genealogies. Twinning has been especially valuable for research into schizophrenia and other forms of mental illness to discover whether they have a biochemical or hereditary basis.

In any case, the question "Any sets of twins in either of your families?" is one that older prospective parents should treat with care. An alternative may be to wait to conceive until your thirty-seventh year—and its elevated hormone production—is past.

CHAPTER 6

"Negative Population Growth? <u>We</u> Got Nothing But!"

SCENE: *France, 1582. Each winter for six years King Henry III and his queen walked the road on pilgrimage from Paris to Chartres, wearing penitential robes, praying for an heir. "They offered a silver-gilt statue of Notre Dame weighing 50 pounds, with the object of having lineage which might succeed to the throne." Their prayers went unanswered; the House of Valois died out.*

SCENE: *a tent in the Mideast, about 1500 B.C. And as Abraham fell prostrate, he laughed and said to himself, "Shall a son be born to one who is a hundred years old? Shall Sara, who is ninety, bear a child?"*

Sara was listening inside the entrance to the tent. So Sara laughed to herself and said, "Now that I am grown old, and my husband is old, shall I then have pleasure?"

The Lord said to Abraham, "Why does Sara laugh, saying, 'Shall I indeed bear a child, though I am old?' Is anything too wonderful for the Lord? At this time next year I will return to you, and Sara shall have a son."

Contemporary scene: living room in Westchester County, north of Manhattan. Winter night. A group of women and one or two husbands gather for a monthly meeting to discuss their common problem and their program to help others suffering from it.

SANDRA: "It's a shock to find out you can't have a child after assuming you could because everybody else does."

BETTY: "It affects 15 percent of U.S. couples. That's one out of seven. But people are so worried about birth control and abortion that they can't imagine how failure to have children also hurts."

JEAN: "If you want to pay 10 or 12 thousand dollars, a lawyer will 'find' you a baby to adopt. With abortion, we can't even find adoptable babies anymore."

Begun in 1970 by Loretta Fine, this group now has 60 members, a regular newsletter, a list of helpful doctors, a hotline number to receive calls from desperate couples as far away as Texas. Membership costs $10 per year. They are organized and sympathetic.

Their histories differ. Some were fortunate enough to find an adoptable child before abortion became legal in New York State. Others conceived a child after a full infertility "workup," including precisely timed intercourse along with much strain and frustration. Some have considered artificial insemination. The women support each other through the battery of tests and the emotional trial of awaiting results.

"But how do we help *more* people? Even if we use our money to donate a piece of equipment to a doctor's office, how many will that help?"

"People are so embarrassed to talk at first. . . . How do we bring out all the . . . *closet queens?"* We laugh. Infertile couples are hardly a persecuted minority, but it is true that most Americans worry more about controlling their fertility than encouraging it.

"Yes, if we can help even one couple have a healthy baby, we're doing our job."

Anita Weiss, one member of the group's board and now an active mother of three youngsters, says, "We want to give people hope by giving them direction. I'm sure most couples can be helped. It's a question of educating them to seek treatment. You need to seek the very best help. It takes a doctor with a lot of patience."

Most meetings help by answering questions, comparing information from articles, books, personal experience. At one session Dr. Charles Debrovner, director of ob-gyn at French Polyclinic Medical Center, New York City, came to speak. A sandy-haired, informally dressed man, he settled into an armchair and spoke without notes for nearly an hour.

"You wanted to know how to speed up the process of infertility study for a couple. Well, tests must be done at several times during the woman's menstrual cycle, not just once. But remember a doctor deals with people, not just biologic specimens. He needs time to judge and counsel both members of a couple to determine how dedicated they are to solving the problem."

Dr. Debrovner described some commonly available tests, such as the postcoital (Huehner) that checks a woman's cervical mucus for presence of sperm, or the gas insufflation (Rubin) test to determine whether Fallopian tubes are open by passing carbon dioxide through the uterus into them. This test can be painful; one woman who had it winces. An infertility workup also determines whether thyroid or endocrine problems are preventing regular ovulation.

Dr. Debrovner also discussed male tests to observe and determine sperm count and mobility and mentioned a new possibility of interest to older men. This is varicocele (last syllable pronounced "seal")—surgery on the prostrate gland to tie off swollen veins that can prevent full ejaculation, even sperm production. Dr. Debrovner believes it has some value but, like surgery on the female organs, risks the formation of scar tissue that, being inelastic, can also hamper fertility.

Finally, he answered questions about sperm banks, artificial insemination, drug side effects, miscarriage, and people with psychological infertility, such as women who can have a regular cycle *except* when they attempt pregnancy, and husbands who can be potent except on the day of ovulation. "Psychological problems are hard on both men and women but probably harder on the man—they represent more of a failure for him."

Dr. Debrovner offered friendly suggestions. "Couples may postpone pregnancy, never dreaming that when they do want a child, they may prove infertile for any number of reasons. That's why infertility can be so devastating. When people marry, they should not ask, 'How old do I want to be for my first child?' but rather 'How old will I be when I have my *last* child?'

"Infertility is neither a male nor a female problem. It's a problem of infertile *mating*. If we must assign percentages, it's probably 60 percent a female problem, 40 percent male."

Because older couples have much less fertile time left than younger ones for tests, drugs, or new sexual techniques, they need even faster answers. If either or both of you as a couple are undergoing fertility treatment and feel distraught, puzzled, or frustrated at progress or merely seek further information, the Westchester group's name and address are United Infertility Organization, P.O. Box 23, Scarsdale, New York 10583. Their answering service number is (914)723-1687. If you leave your name and address, a group member will contact you.

Is there a point at which a couple should give up hope for a child? Like other pregnancy-related topics, this is a matter of opinion. Dr. Debrovner's answer is indirect. "It's like the great American ballgame. When the team is losing, you change managers."

Dr. Shepard Aronson of New York University Medical Center estimates that a woman's "chances of conceiving at 40 are about half those of a woman 35 or under. Anatomically and physically speaking, the mature woman produces either no more eggs or essentially infertile ones. After 45, the chances of conceiving are very low indeed. The oldest woman I know was about 47 when she bore a living child."

The average fertility workup takes 3 to 4 months, followed by 6 to 12 months for further diagnosis and treatment. Chances of successful pregnancy following workup are 20 to 50 percent, or approximately one out of three couples who have sought help after a year of previous inability to conceive. Even the average fertile couple needs 4 to 6 months to achieve pregnancy; most women's eggs are thought to vary in fertility from month to month.

The odds are considerable. Each sperm—only 1/6000 inch diameter, 1/500 inch length—must travel 250,000 times that length to traverse the cervix (1 inch) and uterus (3 to 4 inches) and enter one of the 4-inch Fallopian tubes in which fertilization occurs. Most sperm enter the wrong tube—the one without the egg—or die along the way, but some are known to make the total upstream trip in less than an hour.

The egg, the human body's largest cell, is only 1/200 inch; this is one-quarter the size of the period ending this sentence. Each Fallopian tube is the width of a broom straw and works as follows:

> The inner lining of the tube is exquisitely delicate, consisting of a velvety surface on which there are countless tiny hairlike structures, called cilia. These constantly move in the direction of the uterus, weaving the egg toward its resting place. It is against this current that the sperm must swim to meet and merge with the egg at the furthest end of the tube. (From Sherwin Kaufman, *New Hope for the Childless Couple* [Simon & Schuster, 1970].)

The fertility specialist Dr. Robert Hotchkiss believes, "Failure to conceive is more apt to be due to lowered fertility of both partners than to absolute sterility of either husband or wife." And older couples are most apt to suffer lower fertility from multiple causes. Common ones are:

1. *Injury* to male or female reproductive organs from radiation, accidents, surgery, venereal disease.

2. Male *physical defects,* such as testicular tumor, diabetes, enlarged prostate glands. Female physical defects —blocked Fallopian tubes (30 to 40 percent of infertility), fibroid tumors in older women, deformed hips or pelvis.

3. *Functional defects.* Male and female problems with the endocrine system—pituitary, adrenal, thyroid glands —or with gonads (ovaries or testes). Female failure to ovulate (causes 5 to 15 percent of infertility). Male failure to ejaculate enough sperm of sufficient quality or quantity (causes 30 to 40 percent of infertility).

4. *Poor health,* lack of energy from inadequate nutrition or other causes. Dr. Marie Warner, a New York gynecologist, notes: "Of 1,010 couples I treated for infertility, 90 percent had a basal metabolism below normal." Thyroid insufficiency is one cause of low basal metabolism.

5. *Emotional problems.* Psychologists often summarize this crudely as "rejection of the male or female role."

Nevertheless, the difficulties of trying to achieve or continue pregnancy amid stress caused by job, financial, or marital problems, illness of other children or one's own parents, and love-making regulated by the thermometer, calendar, or test tapes should not be underestimated. A history of involuntary infertility is a history of frustration.

6. *Incomplete, inadequate, or mistimed sexual relations.* The following is incredible, but it happened in this century. In the late 1960s Dr. Warner reported that during 45 years of medical practice, she had seen "more than 500 married virgins, many of whom were completely unaware that their marriage had never been properly consummated." One of them was 44 years old, 26 years married. "I immediately discovered that she still had an intact hymen and probably had never attained full consummation of her marriage."

I assume these were "normal" married women without noticeable physical or psychiatric problems. This in our era of supposed sexual revolution, Masters and Johnson, and female potential for multiple orgasm as described in Dr. Mary Jane Sherfey's *The Nature and Evolution of Female Sexuality*.

Concerning 50 of these women who continued consultation, Dr. Warner adds: "Non-consummation was unquestionably the *only* cause of their so-called 'sterility' because as soon as they had been informed in proper management of the sex act, they promptly became pregnant."

Compared with young people, older couples are more apt to have lacked proper sex education. Middle-aged men and women, at least with their spouses, may be shyer about abandoning accustomed techniques, whether satisfying or not, to try new positions or ideas. For an older woman especially, retraining herself to take any sexual initiative after a lifetime of programmed passivity may threaten both her and her husband.

Often I hear, "If a marriage is good, the husband and wife can work out any problem." The converse, however, seems equally true: If the marriage, the meeting, and the mating had been good, the problems might not have happened. How to distinguish honestly between cause and effect?

THE SUPER BABY DRUGS—CLOMID AND PERGONAL

It is natural for infertile couples to demand hormones or other drugs. Spectacular results occur regularly now. One chagrined Ohio father of brand-new quintuplets said, "They just kept coming. We weren't expecting anything like this."

In 1973 a Colorado woman, Edna Stanek, 34, considered nearly infertile from puberty onward because she ovulated only once or twice a year, bore sextuplets after Pergonal treatment. Five babies survived, an excellent record. Thirty physicians and nurses from three hospitals attended. Months afterward, Mrs. Stanek summarized her life with five new babies plus a 5-year-old son in one word: "Busy!"

Another Pergonal-treated mother was Geraldine Broderick, who gave birth to nine babies in 1971. Of these, the first human nontuplets ever recorded, two were stillborn. After one week only the baby that had weighed 12 ounces remained alive.

Clomid produces twins at most. Pergonal is so powerful that several eggs mature, and these, when fertilized, may possibly subdivide into new embryos. Pergonal is "human menopausal gonadotropin," first isolated in 1952 from the urine of elderly Roman nuns by an Italian chemist. Pergonal directly stimulates the ovaries. Its superlitterness happens because it bypasses or suppresses the body's normal feedback process. The pituitary is the gland that, among other vital functions, orders the manufacture of estrogen and progesterone that create the menstrual cycle. Usually the ovary signals presence of a single ripe ovum to the pituitary, which responds instantly by producing a hormone that urges the ovum out of the egg follicle and stops maturation of further eggs. Doctors attempt to compensate for the effects of Pergonal by injecting that second hormone (corionic gonadotropin) as soon as lab tests indicate the presence of one mature ovum. The body, however, does not always wait for a lab test. Pergonal can cause cysts of the ovaries, which may rupture and endanger a woman's life.

Another much-publicized and very brave woman was Helen Stevenson Meyner, wife of former New Jersey governor Robert Meyner. She was 41 and he was 61 when their first child was born in 1969. During her thirties Mrs. Meyner had various medical problems, including cancer of the pituitary gland. Radiation successfully killed the tumor, although the process threatened her eyesight and left her infertile. Her childbearing years retreating rapidly, she consulted fertility specialists at Columbia Presbyterian Medical Center, New York City. Treatment with Clomid proved ineffective. Clomid is clomiphene, a synthetic hormone-like drug that encourages the pituitary to release FSH—"follicle stimulating hormone"—which matures the ovum.

Next she was given Pergonal injections. Even Pergonal did not work immediately, so doctors, knowing her other health problems, advised ending treatment. She persisted, begging for one more month of the hormone. Reluctantly they agreed. That very next month she became pregnant and gave birth nine months later. She calls it "my miracle baby at 41."

Since that time, doctors have backed off from liberal use of Pergonal. At least one couple recently won a half-million-dollar suit against the Clomid company, Richardson-Merrill, Inc., of Cincinnati, after birth of a baby with multiple and irreparable defects.

Dr. Edward Stim, a Manhattan gynecologist, advises, "Don't go to drugs until all other methods are exhausted. Wait until you are ready to get pregnant. Don't use them just to prove that a woman can ovulate. Many people who are probably not infertile are using these drugs now."

Here are some of Dr. Stim's data: Of nonovulating women using Clomid, three-fourths will ovulate after use, but only one-fourth will get pregnant. And one-fourth of those will miscarry. This is yet more evidence that female failure to ovulate does not by itself begin to explain infertility. (See Joan's experience with these problems in the next chapter.)

MISCARRIAGE

The sudden hemorrhage of a pregnancy that seemed to be proceeding normally is a fact of life—and death—for many couples. Estimated figures on miscarriage are astounding. According to Dr. Virginia Apgar, only about 30 percent of fertilized eggs ever result in birth of a living infant. Of the remaining 70 percent, 16 percent never divide and form new cells; 15 percent do not continue development; 27 percent do not implant successfully; 11 percent stop developing or abort after the second week of pregnancy. Some of these are called "bad eggs" because they are overripe, deteriorating, or otherwise defective at fertilization.

Of 500,000 total miscarriages yearly in the U.S., an estimated 100,000 are caused by chromosomal disorders. In 1975 Drs. J. and A. Boué of Centre International de l'Enfance, Paris, announced results of research correlating miscarriage and chromosome abnormalities with length of menstrual cycle. Frequency of abnormality in miscarried fetuses was 78 percent of 72 women whose menstrual cycles were longer than 32 days. Of control-group women, who had normal 28-day cycles, 62 percent of fetuses indicated chromosomal abnormalities.

Another researcher, Dr. Ben Z. Taber, analyzed data on live births versus 531 pregnancies ending in miscarriage at Palo Alto Hospital, California, from 1966 to June 1967; 59 (11 percent) of these miscarriages happened to women aged 38 or over. Another 17 percent were unsuccessful ectopic (tubal) pregnancies. Dr. Taber concluded that one-third of the older patients miscarried, compared with 13 percent of women younger than 38.

If a couple has endured three of these spontaneous abortions, genetic counseling and chromosomal study of both husband and wife may be in order. In addition to defective development of the embryo, some early miscarriages occur after the embryo has for some reason ceased developing. The result is a kind of stillbirth.

Doctors differ on the causes and treatment of miscarriage. Some recommend bed rest, hormone shots, psychiatry for emotional problems over parenthood, and cessation of intercourse. Others, like fertility specialist Sherwin Kaufman, declare, "If miscarriage was caused by intercourse, the birth rate would drop to zero."

One doctor, Lyon P. Strean, has made a very logical connection between miscarriage and sudden emotional or physical stress. Under stress the adrenal gland produces cortisone, which he believes can shock or damage the pregnant uterus.

A woman in the real estate business once told me, "You know, I hate cats. When I was six months pregnant for the first time, I walked into our living room one day, and there on our piano sat the neighbors' black cat. I took *one* look at that thing. Next I felt the baby turn over inside me. That was that. A few hours later I lost the baby."

Another theory implicates the neurohormone serotonin. It has been found in abnormal amounts both in women who habitually miscarry and in those under severe emotional stress. It is believed to stimulate uterine contractions until spontaneous abortion occurs.

In a Netherlands study, pregnant women with a history of miscarriage and stillbirth were given no-salt diets to control edema (swelling) and a tendency to eclampsia (high blood pressure toxemia of pregnancy).

> These 12 women had a total of 77 children of whom 55 were born dead. Ten of the women succeeded in having healthy children after they had been put on a saltless diet. Some of the 10 women started to use salt again and once again had interrupted pregnancies. . . . No other therapy was used. (From *Natural Health & Pregnancy* [Rodale Press, 1968].)

Most miscarriages happen before a woman even guesses she is pregnant. She may mistake the sudden bleeding for her usual period. That's why the question "Well, why didn't you *do* something?" from husband or relatives is so infuriating.

One 35-year-old woman told me, "The first week I had what I thought was my normal menstrual period, although I'd been spotting with brown mucus that month. When the bleeding continued into the second week and pieces of white tissue ejected, I went to the doctor. At first he said, 'Yes. This is normal menstrual blood.' Then he found a piece of loose tissue and said, 'What's this? You must be having a miscarriage.' I said, 'That's curious.' I mean, how could I have known? I was never pregnant before. I must have been about six weeks pregnant."

HOW MANY AND WHEN?

Most medical advisers on infertility or pregnancy assume for some reason (probably because it's simpler and avoids emotional factors) that husband and wife have an equal desire to achieve or continue pregnancy. In my opinion, this is not the reality of many contemporary marriages.

A younger woman, for example, married to an older husband, may not at all feel her "time is running out," that she must produce immediate babies so he can avoid "being an old man" to his children. An older husband, already supporting teen-agers from a previous marriage, may be uninterested in a second wife's yearning for her own family. And what a couple agrees on before marriage, assuming they discussed childbearing, may not become what one or the other needs two or five years into the stress of daily life and work together. Birth of a child with severe problems may encourage one optimistic parent to try again, while it altogether discourages the other. Even within a "good" marriage, arguments over the quality, quantity, and timing of children occur.

If you desire children but your spouse does not— at least yet:

1. Try to agree on a *compromise* period for use of your ordinary method of birth control, followed by a period of attempting pregnancy. Be patient with your partner during these periods. Your sexual life as a couple is important, but it need not overwhelm every other aspect of your life together.

2. Try not to nag or hint constantly. You may feel you'll die unless you have a new baby to cuddle or show off this time next year, but your aura of tension and non-negotiable demand will only depress, anger, or mystify your partner. She or he may be preoccupied with work or health problems for which *you* seem to offer little sympathy. Be reasonable.

3. Remember that learning to want to do anything from scuba diving to new sex techniques depends on motivation—and that depends on maturation. Try to discover, without belittling, what the hesitation over par-

enting is. Don't be surprised that even for a 35- or 40-year-old adult, the reason lies squarely in the inadequacies of his (her) own rearing or even in fear of a child's inevitable helplessness.

A speech therapist said to me, "You know, I hated therapy with children when I first started working. Then I had two of my own, and I relaxed. The trouble had been that I was just plain scared of kids with problems. My sister was so close to me in age that I'd never been responsible for a child before I had my own."

Elie Wiesel, survivor of the Nazi concentration camps, didn't father a child until he was 40; the world seemed too fearsome a place. In Helen Meyner's words: "It takes maturity to bring up a child in this world we're living in."

When you don't but your partner does desire parenthood:

1. For first timers: If ignorance or fear are your stumbling blocks, try to learn more about babies. Day-care centers or families in your neighborhood or building will appreciate your male or female services to baby-sit or take their kids for some afternoons of hiking, fishing, or community events. Divorced parents especially yearn for help.

2. If you doubt the stability of your marriage, your own health or finances, try to make your partner see that achieving these priorities is as essential to you as a new or first baby is to him (her). See whether you can arrange nonthreatening marriage or sex counseling, take better care of your health, adjust your career or work load, to assure your partner that pregnancy will be a possibility, if not now, then later.

3. Remember that learning to want to do anything manners already in the neighborhood! The "perfect child" is a myth created by perfectionists.

4. If you are worried about age, remember, to a child, *anyone* over 21 is already "old"! It is your gift of spirit and energy that will interest your baby—not the number of your years or your wrinkles.

For both of you:

If infertility or some other medical, genetic, or emotional problem proves insurmountable, investigate adoption or foster care. Many thousands of American children (although very few infants) are still available to foster parents.

Avoid talk of "blame" or "failure." Few situations are entirely or only one partner's fault. Remember you were a couple *before* you lacked children, and with tolerance, patience, and love you will retain your life as a couple with —or without—children. Many parents will envy all the activities you as a childless couple still have time, money, or energy to enjoy.

BOY OR GIRL?

For all prospective parents embryo transplantation, test-tube fertilization, artificial wombs, and cloning (asexual reproduction) are subjects of much controversy and interest. For the 1970s embryo transplants and artificially induced multiple births have become the medical newsmakers that heart transplants were during the Sixties.

In 1974 Representatives Edward Koch of New York and Tim Lee Carter of Kentucky introduced a bill to establish further federal research programs in fertility, sterility, and the reproductive process at new treatment centers. In 1975 Congress reapproved research on embryos (conception to 3 months) and fetuses (3 to 9 months), following a year's ban while a committee had studied legal and ethical implications. Such research is now legal, provided it meets four criteria: mother's consent; intent of the work is to help the fetus; the aborted fetus is too young to survive; and a national review board has been set up to consider questionable cases, presumably before doctors take action in any particular case.

Amniocentesis for chromosomal or other defects is not considered fetal research since it works only with cast-off cells and does not directly touch the fetus.

In Dr. Aubrey Milunsky's words: "The ethical problems in prenatal diagnosis almost pall in comparison to the controversial issues surrounding present and future *in vitro* (test tube) fertilization of human ova or the development of clonal man." Doctors joke a lot about cloning; it involves, in the same individual, replacing the nucleus of an egg cell with the nucleus of another cell that contains the full (instead of halved) complement of chromosomes.

"If we can do it with tadpoles or carrots, why not make 2,000 copies of Raquel Welch?"

Current or longtime laborers in these fields, however, have gotten into deep trouble as well as deep research. In 1974 British doctors Douglas Bevis, Patrick Steptoe, and Robert Edward were reputed to have conceived at least three children in test tubes from three women's ova and husbands' sperm, then reimplanted the embryos. Three healthy babies were thus born of three women with blocked or diseased Fallopian tubes—a kind of triple miracle. The resulting storm of criticism and the danger of producing genetic defects caused two of the doctors, including Bevis, who actually did the implanting, to retire from research.

In this country Dr. Landrum Shettles of Columbia University and the New York Fertility Research Foundation did the research that resulted in a Florida couple's suing Columbia Presbyterian Hospital for $1.5 million. The director of ob-gyn, Dr. Raymond L. Vande Wiele, upset about embryo research, destroyed the embryo belonging to Doris Del Zio. It had been fertilized with Mr. Del Zio's sperm and was awaiting implantation. The Del Zios had already spent $15,000 and had failed to achieve successful pregnancy via other methods.

Dr. Shettles also has used a tested method of sex selection to help couples achieve birth of the desired sex. Until the 1960s people had to be satisfied with the usual nearly 50–50 chance of having either a girl or a boy. Many folkloric methods have, of course, been tried, usually to achieve birth of boys. Some have involved placing the bed in a north-south direction, drinking wine and lion's blood mixed by an alchemist, taking an ax to bed, awaiting a north wind, letting a little boy step on the bride's hands.

In 1905 Dr. N. M. Stevens studied mealworms (fed to zoo animals) and saw the smaller Y chromosome that produces males. The ova of mealworms all contain 10 large chromosomes, as do one-half the mealworm sperm cells. He reasoned that it is the other half of mealworm sperm containing 9 large and 1 small (Y) chromosome that produces male mealworms.

So it is that fathers from Adam onward have determined the sex of every baby ever born by contributing either an X- or a Y-bearing sperm. The sex of mealworms and humans is similarly determined and the process, while random, is now controllable.

Many people investigated the problem. One mistake was to work with dead human sperm, whose magnified heads, whether X or Y, all appear the same size.

Dr. Shettles tells about one night in the early Sixties. "I'd decided to examine some *living* sperm cells under a phase contrast microscope." This technique silhouettes them with light. He slowed them down with carbon dioxide, and immediately he noticed the sperms had two different sizes and shapes. "I was so excited that I ran upstairs and grabbed the first lab technician I could find. I had to show somebody what I'd found." Small, fast, round-headed "androsperms" produce boys. Slower, larger, oval-headed "gynosperms" create girls.

One of Dr. Shettles' rare and prize exhibits is a series of photos of "nothing but" androsperm from a man whose family for almost 275 years has produced nearly all boys. Two girls managed somehow to get born, although even they displayed "marked hirsutism [body hair] and masculinity."

One of Dr. Shettles' next experiments was to turn both kinds of sperm loose in capillary tubes containing cervical and vaginal secretions. This time it was like "watching the races at Belmont." When the secretions were more acidic than alkaline, gynosperms prevailed. Their larger size protected them longer from the acid. In the absence of acids, androsperms could use their one advantage—speed and agility of the small head mounted on a long tail.

For couples planning a child, the doctor advises, "If the first intercourse of the month takes place right at ovulation time, when cervical fluid increases tenfold and is very alkaline, the male sperm will race through like a cab going down Broadway on a green light." However, if intercourse takes place two or three days before ovulation, most male sperms will die awaiting the egg.

"For the female sperm, it's like flying into LaGuardia on a foggy night. They have to hover around and wait for the signal. Then they zoom right in."

Here are Dr. Shettles' rules for a girl:

1. Cease intercourse two to three days (36 or more hours) before ovulation. No abstinence from intercourse is necessary prior to this date.

2. Determine ovulation date or hour with a special ther-

mometer or with a fertility test tape kit available in drug-
stores or from Weston Laboratories Inc., Ottawa, Illinois
61779.

3. Before each intercourse the woman should douche
with an acid solution of two tablespoons white vinegar to
a quart of water.

4. The woman should avoid orgasm, which increases the
flow of alkaline solutions.

5. Use the face to face, "missionary position" to ensure
that sperms will be deposited in the acid environment of
the vagina rather than right at the mouth of the cervix.

6. Shallow penetration by the male is recommended.

For a boy:

1. Cease intercourse from the beginning of the monthly
cycle until the exact day of ovulation, including 7 hours
after ovulation.

2. The woman should precede each intercourse with an
alkaline douche—two tablespoons baking soda to a quart
of water.

3. Female orgasm is desirable.

4. Vaginal penetration from the rear is the recommended position to deposit sperm directly at the cervix.
Deep penetration is recommended.

For older couples, conditions appear to favor girls. Dr.
Shettles says,

> The sperm count of some males declines with age,
> and this can result in more female offspring. Simi-
> larly, as a woman ages . . . the quality and quantity
> of her cervical secretions, which tend to be alkaline,
> diminish over the years. This deterioration tends to
> favor female offspring. And it is true that older cou-
> ples do produce more female offspring than do
> younger people. One study showed that women of
> about 15, 20, 30, and 40 years of age had offspring
> with sex ratios of 163, 120, 112, and 91 males, re-
> spectively, for every 100 females. The older woman,
> however, if she wants male offspring, can overcome
> this disadvantage by using the alkaline douche and
> timing procedures.

If you as a couple worry foremost about decreased fertility and conceiving any child at all, Dr. Shettles' racy similes may have annoyed you. Discuss these recommendations with your doctor or fertility specialist and follow his supervision.

And how reliable is this timing-plus-douching method?

Average couples with regular menstrual cycle and no unusual problems show clinical results of 80 to 90 percent success in achieving the desired sex. If conception fails to occur after 3 or 4 months and you desire a girl, Dr. Shettles recommends moving to a 2 1/2-day interval, then to 2 days before ovulation. Even at 2 days, a girl will likely be conceived.

One of my interviewees was already the mother of 3 children when she gave birth to a son at 40. She wrote me, "I wanted a boy and became pregnant when my chances for a boy were the biggest. My husband and I were very happy." She had read the article in *Look* magazine in which Dr. Shettles' rules first appeared.

During 1975 two new methods for detecting ovulation were announced. They should soon be commercially available to interested couples. One is test tapes that register the amount of the enzyme alkaline phosphatase in a woman's saliva. As her body temperature rises with ovulation, so does the enzyme level. Chemist Raymond O. Foster developed the tapes. Dr. Albert B. Losincz announced the method at an American Chemical Society meeting in Washington, D.C.

Dr. Carl Schleicher, head of the Mankind Research Foundation, also in Washington, has developed a device called the ovulometer. The size of a cigarette package, it detects a woman's fertile period by measuring voltage given off by her body, probably again correlated with her temperature rise. It is for home use. Several physicians (and one priest) have endorsed its reliability, especially in conjunction with the rhythm method of birth regulation.

An old-fashioned viewpoint maintains that if couples are not ready to accept what they get in the sex of their child, then they're not ready for parenthood. A newer approach indicates that older couples with perhaps only one chance at parenthood deserve all the help they can get to assure a baby of the sex they want.

CHAPTER 7

How to Do Everything You Want—<u>and</u> Raise a Family

JOAN MARRIED LATE. SHE WAS 37 AND HER husband, Jay, 39. After examination and testing by two fertility specialists (whose diagnoses differed), she became pregnant and had her first child, Susan, at 40. Her next pregnancy ended in an early miscarriage. When she was 42, she gave birth to a second daughter, Rebecca.

Joan summarizes the whole experience of achieving three pregnancies after 40 as "pushing the limits of the possible!"

When I interviewed her in person, by phone and letter over a period of several months, the children were about 3 1/2 and 1 1/2. Besides child care and running a home, Joan was finishing the academic year as a high school teacher and the next semester began studies for an M.A. degree in counseling. A busy woman, she has what she calls "a two-career life," including the hours of night duty that small or ailing children require.

Despite the major upheavals in marriage and work that new parenthood can entail, she and Jay have coped well with the duties and difficulties.

"Jay and I were extremely happy when I learned I was

pregnant with Susan. We married in our late thirties and had difficulty conceiving that first time. I finally went to a fertility specialist, or rather to two of them. The first was a disaster. He came highly recommended by the local doctor. For some reason he had developed a reputation as a gynecologist in this rather isolated community. Although half the antiquated tests he gave me indicated that I did ovulate, at least sometimes, he insisted I did not because one particular sign he was seeking did not occur.

"When I mentioned the fact that my temperature charts also showed elevation indicating ovulation, he attributed this to 'a slip of your hand in making the chart, due to eagerness to conceive.' His conclusion: My only hope was fertility drugs, with the consequent 20 percent risk of multiple birth.

"We decided to seek another opinion before taking this risk. However, I suffered nightmares about multiple births, one time seven babies squirming in my tummy, then five healthy quintuplets all decked out in layettes, with me rushing around giving five bottles, etc. Each time I awoke in a cold sweat and felt exhausted, drained, by this possibility.

"Fortunately we live close to Manhattan and could consult Dr. Stewart Marcus, then head of the Fertility Clinic at New York Hospital and one of the experts on this subject in the U.S. Though haughty, as most male gynecologists seem to be, he was optimistic about the chances. He recognized from the previous tests the very simple evidence that indeed I did ovulate though not regularly. He concluded that the problem was not ovulation but possible partial blockage of one or both Fallopian tubes, which prevented the egg from traveling its normal route.

"Fertility drugs then were not required and would not have solved the problem. I stress this so that other couples may beware. Dr. Marcus, of course, obtained my reports from the other doctor, so I didn't need to repeat the original series of tests. And he had far more sophisticated methods to test the tubes, which probably had a therapeutic effect in clearing blockage. The tubes, in fact, did not show up blocked during the Rubin test, although one was more open than the other.

"One month after that test was administered and before we could go farther, I found myself pregnant."

I wondered whether Joan and Jay had sought genetic

counseling before or in addition to the fertility treatment. She answered, "Genetic counseling and its related tests were not common in my area during my first or second pregnancy. Jay and I were both concerned about the child's normality but did not talk about it to each other until after the birth. He was *excessively* concerned that I do everything to avoid miscarriage. This caused some tension between us.

"One piece of helpful information I picked up only after the first birth was that studies show that a retardation-malformation rate of one per 10 pregnancies applied only to couples over 40 who had been long married and, therefore, had infrequent intercourse. Couples more recently married or having more frequent intercourse did not have that rate of deformed children."

I asked Joan about others' reactions to her pregnancy, and how her early pregnant months compared with the later months. "Everybody seemed happy for us but also apprehensive about me and whether the first baby would be normal. . . . Psychologically I continued to be delighted and proud of being with child. Three weeks before Susan's due date, we moved without qualms to a co-op apartment.

"Physically, however, from the seventh month onward, I found myself exhausted one hour after rising until I started the diet and supplements, especially brewer's yeast, recommended by Adelle Davis in *Let's Have Healthy Children.* That made an enormous difference and I felt good again until the end."

Later, Joan repeated that "the importance of a good diet, both for me and the babies" was the most important lesson she had learned through pregnancy.

I asked about Joan's choice of an obstetrician, hospital, and education for the first birth. While she and her husband were highly satisfied with the hospital maternity program, they were much less so with the physician. "We chose a doctor associated with a hospital that encourages natural childbirth, parent participation, breast-feeding. This doctor was a bit nervous about my age (40) but otherwise treated me routinely. Like other ob-gyn men I have dealt with, he seemed to have little respect for women. I did much reading but didn't bother trying to discuss it with him. Since I was particularly interested in the nutritional aspect of pregnancy, I adopted Adelle Davis's recommendations for vitamin supplements and continued them because I began to feel much better than when I was taking the multivitamin pill prescribed by the doctor. He did not agree with this, so finally I just did it from desperation to maintain my energy in the later months.

"The hospital I chose is outstanding for its maternity program. The nursing care was marvelous, encouraging of natural childbirth. I used the Lamaze method, although I could have chosen not to go natural if I'd wanted. Jay attended natural childbirth classes with me, directed my daily exercises, and assisted me throughout that first labor, which lasted 17 hours. He was present for the delivery and was first to hold the baby. . . . Even after visiting hours, this hospital allows a father to fetch his baby from the nursery, play with it, and get to know it for an hour each evening.

"Because of such long labor, a forceps delivery, and more stitches than usual, it took me months to feel well again after this first birth. The saddleblock injection alone gave me a dreadful headache that lasted two weeks."

I asked Joan's opinion of delivery at home with a midwife or doctor in attendance. "If I were younger and had no sign of complication, I might do it. However, because of age, I wouldn't take such a chance myself."

Despite Joan's difficulty at conceiving the first child, her second and third conceptions happened easily. "The whole childbearing mechanism was in excellent working order after the first baby." Although her second pregnancy miscarried before two months, she soon found herself pregnant again. "My third pregnancy proceeded normally. Although it was much easier psychologically than the first had been because we worried less, it was more difficult physically.

"Our second baby, Rebecca, was delivered easily, although I was then 42. I again had natural childbirth, went from start to finish in four hours, and managed well without any anesthesia.

"Because of my age and because I had conceived the previous two times so easily, I had a tubal ligation the same day as the delivery. This has given us much peace of mind ever since. . . ."

I asked Joan some questions about how she and Jay had financed these years of medical and surgical care, and what she thought of her family health insurance policy.

She answered readily. "Blue Cross in New York is shamefully inadequate for maternity benefits. It paid $80 period! Half the doctor's fee was covered. Because our insurance plan paid only a fraction of the doctor's fee for later infant visits, we have switched to a health insurance plan open to New York City employees. We are very pleased with it."

Joan and I next discussed what she had liked best and least about pregnancy. "It brought a special closeness, joy, and anticipation of Jay and me. With the second baby, our first child also joined our anticipation. . . . And maternity clothes are comfortable. I've always enjoyed roomy uniforms! I liked least the physical discomfort, especially toward the end."

BABIES AND CAREERS

Joan is a woman who has adjusted to parenthood after spending the previous 20 years "in career." She did it by changing her field of work and in response to the pressure to earn more to help support the growing children.

"After Susan's birth I did freelance editing and writing at home, connected with the job I'd held for two years. That was great. It involved a textbook-workbook series for which I wrote one textbook and two workbooks. However, this series and other projects I'd worked on gradually ended. Although such work does combine well with caring for small children, I finally found it too sporadic and too lonely.

"Youngsters can demolish a work life. Theirs is so small a world, with such immediate needs. As for another real career, I know I must wait until they're both in nursery school. Recently I've taught school, but since this is currently a shrinking field, I'm switching to related work. I feel I have to be sure of my employability in case anything happened to Jay. It will be 17 years, for instance, before the girls are even out of high school."

BABIES AND MARRIAGE

I asked Joan one question that many people wonder about older parents—how easily she and Jay, a college teacher, have incorporated two active youngsters under 5

years old into their daily lives. The process involves negotiation and rapid learning of many new skills.

"Babies, especially the first one, create a revolution in
a marriage. Jay has always been good about sharing the
work of the children—changing diapers, helping at meals,
bath time, etc.

"After the first difficult birth, the housework, however,
was really a drag, besides the fact that we were still getting unpacked and settled. Since I was now home all the
time, Jay didn't feel *he* should have to share cooking and
shopping, as he'd done when we were both working. Neither did he approve of my getting help with the cleaning,
as I'd also done previously. He thought I should be able
to manage it; his mother always had.

"Well, things came to a crisis. Eventually he agreed to
having a woman come and help one-half day per week.
Since then, we've had few problems in this area.

"Some months before the second baby was due, we
moved again because there was no outside place for children to play in our co-op. We bought a house. Sooner or
later children do force you to think about a house. Neither
of us looked forward to the extra work, but the benefits
seemed worth it. Since there's always plenty to do around
the house, Jay now has his fair share without doing
'housework.' I still have the woman one-half day per
week.

"We got a freezer and food plan to reduce shopping,
and Jay built me a big storage chest for buying food by
the case. These, plus the luxury of milk delivery while the
babies were small, have also minimized shopping.

"It has developed that Jay enjoys home-improvement
work and has unsuspected skills. The effort is even a
change of pace for him that he enjoys. Neither of us expected that happy turn of events.

"I've found that one full day per season of gardening,
plus other odd moments for seeding and weeding, gives
one the feeling and pleasure of being a bit in touch with
nature. Jay does the grass and hedges. We have mostly
perennials, so the modest care we give our modest garden
is rewarding. And houses are great for kids. So here we
are.

"However, we've not kept up sufficiently with our other
interests, particularly cultural, but we live in hope that this
will improve."

Joan remarked that the most important thing she's learning through parenthood is "tremendous respect for other parents, especially of large families, who do a good job."

I quoted a few sentences from Dr. Spock's *Redbook* column (September, 1969) on older and younger parents to obtain her reaction:

> A mother still in her teens or just out of them is emotionally less apt to be tolerant of the behavior of a child, less apt to enjoy it, just because she is too close to childhood. . . . The older woman, thoroughly secure in her maturity, can enjoy those special charms of children that are expressions of their immaturity—their ingenuousness, their wonderment, their spontaneity, their enthusiasm.

"Jay and I do enjoy the girls more than many young couples might. I also think that because we did many things before we married and had children, we enjoy rather than resent the time we must give them. We wouldn't mind being five years younger to keep up with them, though! We often find ourselves really exhausted. After 40 it takes longer to get rested up. We have been mistaken for the children's grandparents. . . .

"One problem is that I keep expecting Susan to act older, compared with the baby. I expect a level of maturity she's not capable of yet."

"How's your level of patience and tolerance?" I asked.

"I never had much! But it has been enlarged. However, if I don't get a midday break, it declines rapidly as the hours wear on."

"If men could get pregnant—?"

"There would be fewer children in the world."

"Motherhood is—?"

"Rewarding/trying/demanding/exhausting—and often fun!"

CHAPTER 8

Some Do's on Diet
and Drugs

"I can't wait till the baby is born so I don't have to eat a balanced diet anymore!"

FOR THIS BOOK I ATTENDED THE REGULAR prenatal classes given by a public health nurse at the local hospital. The first few meetings included a film, explanations of anatomy and physiology, and a tour of the delivery room. All these were well attended by a group of expectant couples.

On nutrition evening, however, we became a tiny group in a big room. Besides the teacher, just two people appeared—myself and the woman whose views on diet are evident in the above quotation.

Despite Americans' interest in preserving health and youth, the subject of diet and nutrition (what you should eat) is considered to be boring compared with discussing meals and snacks (what you like to eat). Many people feel if they've survived this far on some combination of two, three, or more meals a day (breakfast-no breakfast, vitamins-no vitamins, worry or apathy about calories), then they'll survive a few more years.

Doctors commonly prescribe vitamin and mineral supplements now for the general health of both mother and fetus and for special problems (calcium to prevent last-trimester maternal tooth decay). You may experience pregnancy without suffering more than mild twinges of morning sickness or backache. If so, you may wonder what all the fuss is about.

As pregnancy advances, however, you as an older woman or couple may discover you can't continue your usual lifestyle, which may have involved no more than six hours of sleep a night, no breakfast, or a diet lunch. You may be tired, depressed, or irritable, and your spouse may be getting upset. The vitamins your doctor prescribed are not enough. You suspect you should eat more of something else, but you've lost interest in food, let alone creative cooking. What do you do?

First of all, you're not alone. Here are some answers to my question, "What did you like least about your last pregnancy?"

Forty-one-year-old mother of two from Massachusetts: "Nausea! Was nauseous for 6 months."

Forty-two-year-old Long Island mother of five: "I was very big—very uncomfortable. I had a lot of pressure."

New Jersey woman, 37: "Anxious to get it over with. Feeling clumsy—but only with my second pregnancy with a small baby underfoot."

Long Island mother of four: "Losing my shape."

Washington State mother of four: "For me this late pregnancy brought varicose veins and pushed my weight up permanently."

Joan and Alice, the two mothers whom I interviewed in depth (see Chapters 7 and 14), stressed food because their doctors' routine treatment seemed inadequate for their daily energy needs or other problems.

Of her first pregnancy, Joan wrote in chapter 7 on her use of brewer's yeast and the recommendations given in Adelle Davis's books. Joan's doctor did not agree but failed to offer better dietary advice to combat her problem, which was constant fatigue.

"Physically from the seventh month on, I found myself exhausted one hour after rising until I started the diet and supplements recommended by Adelle Davis, especially brewer's yeast. That made an enormous difference and I felt good until the end.

"My doctor was a bit nervous because of my age (40)

but otherwise treated me routinely. Like most ob-gyn men I have dealt with, he was a male chauvinist with very little respect for women. I did much reading but didn't bother trying to discuss it with him. I was particularly interested in the nutritional aspect of pregnancy. I read Adelle Davis's books and eventually adopted her recommendation for vitamin supplements listed in *Let's Have Healthy Children.* Indeed, I began to feel much better than when on the multivitamin pill prescribed by the doctor. He did not agree with this, so finally I just did it from desperation to maintain my energy."

According to urine tests Dr. Berk has made on his patients, vitamin tablets (whether natural or synthetic) are excreted in the urine in such large amounts that he feels they are useless to the pregnant woman. He advises getting vitamins through the choice of proper foods. He does prescribe mineral or iron supplements when needed, however.

Alice was 42 when her son was born. She says that after the birth she felt "great," had lost excess weight, and was trimmer than she'd been since age 13. One doctor who examined her remarked that she had a body like a woman of 30. Her interest in healthful food led her to consult a nutritionist as well as her obstetrician. Here is her advice for pregnancy plus many months of successful breast-feeding:

"I use *Diet for a Small Planet,* the cookbook by Frances Moore Lappé. She believes in complementarity, getting high-quality proteins by combining beans and rice, for example. All essential amino acids are present in her combinations, making them as good or better than meat protein. The problem with much vegetable proteins is that they lack one or another essential amino acid. You have to eat all essential amino acids together for complete protein.

"I do eat very healthy food. When I can organize for myself, I'm practically vegetarian. However, my husband is not. So I decided the human context of the meal is as important as my principles, barring emergency or other reason for strictness."

I asked her if that meant that she ate eggs and cheese but not much meat.

"That's right. Since the birth I've consulted a nutritionist several times who put me on an all-vegetable diet to begin nursing the baby. This stuff about nursing mothers' needing milk and liquids is not true."

Alice chose certain vegetables for specific reasons:

"Green leafy ones are vital for pregnancy and lactation. Things like cabbage, chard, spinach, watercress, broccoli —at least two green vegetables per day. I ate potatoes, brown rice, beans, lentils for protein. After a few weeks I expanded to nuts, cheese, dairy products, two eggs per week."

I asked if she preferred the vegetables raw or cooked.

"Raw are better, but cooked aren't forbidden. Besides the richer vitamins, the advantage of raw is the enzymes aiding digestion that the cooked do not have. If at the same meal you mix raw with cooked, it's good to eat the raw first as salad to increase enzymes.

"This doctor believes in getting most liquids via fruits and vegetables. He allowed me only one teaspoon of cider vinegar and one of honey in a glass of water before breakfast and supper. I drank this gradually before and during the meal. After the first week I added a glass of tea after each meal. No milk to drink.

"He doesn't even recommend juices. He believes the body uses juices better when they're obtained directly from fruit. It takes longer to peel and eat two oranges, compared with drinking a glass of juice, but they do not turn the stomach so suddenly acid."

Alice still consults this doctor because she believes his views for continuing breast-feeding and against starting very young (2-month-old) babies on solid foods are wise and humane. He rapidly solved an infant diarrhea problem—Alice's initial reason for consulting him.

"During the first 2 1/2 months the baby had diarrhea —dirty diapers nine times a day," she told me. "This doctor recommended two ounces of goat's milk twice a day with a half teaspoon of honey right before bed—plus nursing. And in two days that diarrhea cleared up. I used canned condensed goat's milk mixed with water."

Although the nutritionist said Alice could nurse throughout the first year without adding solid foods, she worried about the baby's iron supply. (Breast milk is low in iron, so newborns come equipped with a 6-month body supply.) She began solids at 7 months.

These days you needn't be either a biochemist or a "food faddist" to take a sensible interest in the diet you and your spouse feed yourselves, your unborn child, or other children. However, the usual admonition, "Eat a balanced diet," is neither enlightening nor compelling—unless you know what and why.

At the back of the book (pp. 201–203) you'll find a list of vitamins, minerals, and foods specifically related to pregnancy and birth. These recommendations were adapted from the book *Be a Healthy Mother, Have a Healthy Baby* (Rodale Press, 1973), which details research concerning all nutrients. Probably you neither want nor need to reorganize your total diet. However, incorporating just a few of the easily available items (liver, beans, nuts; yeast and wheat germ on breakfast cereal) may make the difference between several months of health and vigor—or exhaustion and depression.

MALNUTRITION AND/OR OBESITY

Malnutrition is not only or necessarily a disease of the poor. Dr. Mary Ellen Avery, a pediatrician at Johns Hopkins University, said in *Obstetrics-Gynecology News* (June 15, 1969): "As many as 80% of 6,000 mothers in one study had insufficient protein intake. Ironically, the women in this study were not poverty stricken. They had enough to eat—but chose the wrong foods."

By another estimate (National Foundation-March of Dimes, 1972), municipal hospitals reported that between one-third and one-half of women in labor had little or no medical care prior to hospitalization. This almost guarantees inadequate nutrition.

Some research announced during 1975 combined data from a 10-state nutrition study done by the Department of Health, Education and Welfare with data on the nutritional status of U.S. preschool children collected by two universities. Using the 1970 census, a research group led by Dr. Robert B. Livingston, Department of Neurosciences, University of California, San Diego, estimated "the total number of pregnant women in the United States suffering malnutrition serious enough to endanger their babies was more than 945,000. . . . They estimated the number of infants and children in the jeopardized group already born at more than 1,100,000."

If you and your spouse are weight watchers, the topic of recommended gain in pregnancy is crucial to you. Here again you must analyze the merits of conflicting approaches and choose your doctor based on your body type and needs.

Physicians of the last 30 years have advocated modest (17 percent) weight gain—10 to 20 pounds, or no more than a pound a week for the last few months of pregnancy. With growing concern over brain damage and other defects in small birth-weight babies, many doctors today believe the allowable weight gain should be increased.

Most radical is "the Ralph Nader of obstetrics," Dr. Tom Brewer, prenatal clinic director in Richmond, California. He says, "Maternal malnutrition during pregnancy is responsible for the annual death of 30,000 infants and the birth defects of 200,000 children. Metabolic toxemia of late pregnancy is directly caused by malnutrition." Such malnutrition particularly affects two functions of the liver—producing albumin, a protein substance, and initiating the breakdown of excess female hormones from the placenta. Inadequate protein intake and metabolism then result in edema, hypertension, and toxemia.

Dr. Brewer recommends high weight gain, 25 to 50 pounds. "Even if you go to 50 or 60 pounds, it won't hurt you. The average weight gain of a healthy mother is 32 pounds; on a balanced, adequate diet you don't gain too much."

He condemns common means of obstetric management such as diuretics and "diet" (appetite killing) pills. "Millions of women are told not to eat salt during pregnancy. But that's wrong advice. A pregnant woman needs salt just as a pregnant animal does to remain in good health.

"In many clinics, a woman gaining more than the doctor thinks she should is put on a 1,200 to 1,500 calorie low-salt diet, and then when she starts having normal physiologic edema, he brings out the water pills. If she's well nourished, it may not hurt too much, but if the woman is malnourished and he gives her the water pills, it really becomes difficult."

How a woman approaching middle age, with its usual potential for weight gain, can shed 30 to 50 pounds after the birth seems of less concern to Dr. Brewer. However, he is right that pregnancy or lactation are certainly no periods to diet in order to *lose* weight or to compensate for a previous 10 or 20 years of poor eating habits. Perhaps, following the familiar medical principle that balances risk (obesity) against benefit (a healthy baby), he finds obesity the lesser risk.

In the U.S., low birth weight is partly a racial and financial problem. The National Institutes of Health did a large study—55,908 black and white mothers, including about 600 aged 40 or over, surveyed from 1959 to 1965. Published in 1972, the research correlated race with babies' condition:

> In summary, the constant relationship between race and adverse fetal outcome is observed; across age groups, Negro women generally show higher rates than whites with respect to prenatal deaths and increased rates of low birthweight [below 4 1/2 pounds.] The mean birthweights of Negroes are constantly lower than those of whites at every maternal age.

But the dangers of obesity during pregnancy should not be overlooked. It is possible to be both overweight *and* malnourished in the sense of choosing the wrong foods. In some German research reported in *Good Housekeeping* (October, 1974), women of 200 pounds or more produced children with a perinatal death rate of 3.5 percent compared with 1.4 percent for mothers under 160 pounds. Women with serious weight problems also had twice as many miscarriages.

Diet and weight control in pregnant women are important, but to achieve pink, healthy babies, no one should overlook the need for more adequately managed births with more prepared mothers and less anesthesia. Wise choice of birth method (Chapters 15 and 16) becomes crucial.

"I don't know what's the matter. I think I'm broken."
                                        Arthur, 12 years old

Like good nutrition, minimizing the risk of congenital defects is an area in which your knowledge and decisions can help prevent trouble. Defects may be caused by maternal and fetal infection, by mutations triggered by drugs and other substances, or by the birth process itself.

According to Dr. Aubrey Milunsky, congenital malformations cause 10 to 20 percent of all infant deaths. Major deformities, like clubfoot or cleft palate, are noticed immediately. Clubfoot is the most frequent of these malformations—one in 300 births—and affects twice as many boys as girls. However, 20 to 50 percent of deformities, such as problems with perception or muscle coordination, are not noticed until months or years after birth.

The first three months of pregnancy are crucial for preventing defects. A glance at this abbreviated table, basic to the science of embryology, shows why.

Days During Pregnancy	Beginning Formation of
15–25	baby's nervous system
24–36	eyes and limbs
28–45	heart
29–45	ears and nose
36–42	fingers and toes

The dangers from rubella infection or a drug like thalidomide have been well publicized. One of my respondents chose abortion after a rubella infection during her first pregnancy.

When Dr. Virginia Apgar was vice-president for medical research of the National Foundation-March of Dimes, she said, "The placenta is a sieve. Almost everything ingested or injected into the mother can be expected to reach the fetus within a few minutes." Certain drugs appear to settle in even greater concentrations in the fetal brain, heart muscle, or other organs than in the mother, and the placenta's transfer capacity increases, rather than decreases, as the months pass.

Some of Dr. Apgar's figures: A baby with a "significant birth defect" is born every two minutes in the U.S. This is one of every 16 babies—about one-quarter million per year. Many physicians consider such defects the greatest unmet problem in child care today.

Most congenital malformations occur without observable chromosomal or biochemical evidence in the prenatal period. So it is up to you, with your doctor, to do what you can to prevent these defects.

SIX SUGGESTIONS FOR A HEALTHY BABY

1. *Avoid chest or abdominal x-rays* during pregnancy. Ask for a lead apron during dental x-rays.

2. *Re-examine your intake of all chemicals,* including prescription and other drugs. Most drugs are combinations of many substances. A chemical is anything whose ingredients are absorbed through the digestive system or the skin—sleeping pills, cold remedies, suppositories, deodorants, face lotions, lipsticks, hair spray or household cleaners in aerosol cans, wines and liquors, artificially colored soft drinks.

It seems sensible during pregnancy to reduce your intake of any chemical or additive substance about which a health controversy has already occurred. *Prevention* magazine regularly reports on tests and laws involving many substances. It was one of the first to warn the public about the recently banned Red Dye No. 2. Taking excessive amounts of vitamins and minerals instead of eating nutritious foods is also potentially harmful.

During 1975 an Australian study even implicated regular (once a week) use of aspirin in stillbirths and other pregnancy problems. However, some drugs are proper during pregnancy to treat chronic or acute maternal diseases that would otherwise cause prematurity, fetal infection, lowered fetal oxygenation. Examples are insulin for diabetes; digitalis for heart disease; certain antibiotics for pneumonia, diarrhea, high fever, urinary tract infection; certain antinausea drugs; treatment for phlebitis or tuberculosis.

3. *Consider whether you should continue to rinse, dye, or bleach your hair.*

Twenty million Americans do. These chemicals can be absorbed through your scalp. Through industry lobbying, hair dyes were and are exempt from the original 1938 Food, Drug, and Cosmetic Act and from succeeding legislation. Hair-dye chemicals concentrate in the urine of humans. Research is now linking these chemicals with the high rate of bladder cancer in beauticians and with breast cancer.

Dr. Bruce N. Ames, professor of biochemistry at the University of California, Berkeley, has provided the most damaging evidence, although his test methods have been attacked as "oversensitive." In an April 4, 1975, letter to the *New York Times,* Dr. Ames wrote:

> We have developed a rapid and sensitive test (using bacteria and animal tissue) for identifying mutagens (chemicals that damage the genetic material), which is now in use in a large number of drug and industrial companies throughout the world. . . . We find that 150 out of 169 oxidative-type hair dyes tested, most of the semi-permanent type dyes tested, nine of the components of hair dyes, and several oxidation products of hair dye ingredients are mutagenic.

The *Times* commented:

> Though the findings are inconclusive, laboratory tests have raised the possibility that hair dyes used by 20 million Americans can cause cancer and birth defects. . . .
> Because many of the chemicals in the hair dyes are aromatic amines and diamines, closely related to substances that are known carcinogens, Dr. Ames concluded that "each of the hair dye compounds we have found to be mutagenic has a high probability of proving to be a carcinogen."

Disease and/or mutation producers in the environment are called "teratogens," and the study of them, "teratology." This whole field of interrelationship between drugs and heredity is called "pharmacogenetics." According to Dr. Apgar: "Some teratogens can cause a variety of birth defects, depending on the genetic sensitivity and the time during prenatal life it affects the unborn."

When I spoke with Dr. Kurt Hirschhorn of Mt. Sinai Hospital and Medical School, New York City, he mentioned that some people can destroy or detoxify dangerous chemicals entering their bodies. Others lack the proper enzymes; their immunity systems are functioning poorly. He stressed that the effects of many chemicals, such as vinyl chloride (found in most plastics), are cumulative. Female vinyl chloride workers and wives of male workers are now being observed for incidence of tumors, mutations, spontaneous abortions. Another group under study is hospital anesthetists and operating room nurses.

4. *If you own a cat, ask someone else to clean the litter box.* Avoid emptying mousetraps or working garden soil in which pets, especially cats, have defecated. Toxoplasmosis, now thought to be spread by house pets and by eating underdone (less than 140°F. on the meat thermometer) meat, can cause major damage to unborn infants. Over 20 percent of those infected with the virus during the first trimester of pregnancy are born with irreversible defects, including mental retardation, epilepsy, eye damage, hearing loss.

Toxoplasmosis can occur without initial symptoms. A friend is partly but permanently blind in one eye from toxoplasmosis contracted without pain, leaving her with a scarred retina. Once infected, an adult is believed immune to further attacks.

5. *Stop or reduce the amount of your cigarette smoking.*

Most available research contains bad news about smoking. In 1972 a British study reported that babies of mothers who smoked had a 30 percent increased risk of stillbirth, a 26 percent higher risk for perinatal death. In 1973 the *British Medical Journal* reported elevated physical and mental retardation rates for 7- and 11-year-old children whose mothers had smoked at least one-half pack per day during the last half of pregnancy.

In 1975 the *Medical Tribune* quoted Dr. Neville R. Butler, a pediatrician in Bristol, England, who reported a 33 percent increased risk of perinatal death in babies of mothers who smoked. The problem is fetal oxygenation during pregnancy. Dr. Butler found that smoking just one cigarette raises the carbon monoxide in maternal blood by 10 percent, lowers available oxygen, and the effect lasts seven hours.

One woman in the prenatal class told us, "I quit smoking as soon as I found out I was pregnant. For these nine months I know I'm breathing for two."

6. *Learn about the role of Rh factor in pregnancy.*

If you have adequate prenatal care, your doctor will soon take a blood sample and determine whether you are among the 15 percent of white Americans who are Rh negative. This is a race-related problem. Only 5 percent of American blacks are affected (from affected whites' mating with or marrying their ancestors) and practically no Orientals. Rh disease is a hereditary problem. Two Rh negative parents, like two Rh positive parents, need not worry. Problems occur with a negative mother-positive father-positive baby combination, although positive fathers do not always produce positive babies. The Rh+ gene is ordinarily dominant. However, genes are inherited in pairs; individual fathers may be "heterozygotic" for the trait—possess both the dominant Rh+ gene and a recessive Rh— gene. Each child of such a father has a 50–50 chance to inherit either the positive or negative factor.

Two hundred and fifty thousand Rh+ babies are born annually to Rh— mothers; 5,000 are stillborn; another 20,000 with Rh birth defects. The condition is treated with immediate blood exchange transfusions into the afflicted baby. A new injection procedure can now prevent Rh incompatibility of the woman and the fetus before maternal antibodies build up during the first pregnancy or birth.

A friend who is Rh negative miscarried her first pregnancy. Following the miscarriage, in addition to immunization, she received an Rh identification card that reads in part, "If I deliver an Rho (D) positive baby (or have a miscarriage), I should be considered as a candidate for RhoGAM. I must receive the injection within 72 hours after the delivery or miscarriage if my protection is to continue."

These injections protect both mother and infant from incompatibility of blood factors unless an older Rh— mother, through repeated births, is already sensitized and has built antibodies that endanger her Rh+ baby. More than 350,000 Rh— mothers receive this vaccine yearly in the U.S.

By this time, confronted with such a variety of dangerous substances, do you feel somewhat paranoid as well as pregnant? You feel blamed if you ignore the risks and yet blamed, or blame yourself, for the bad effects of worrying about them. It's usually amid all the worries that somebody also advises, "Avoid stress during pregnancy!" For example, the French obstetrician Dr. Leboyer believes that pregnant women should read "special newspapers with only good news in them." This is unrealistic, and the women's movement rightly attacks such ignorance-is-bliss plus the pessimism behind it—that accurate information makes people sicker because they are considered too helpless or fragile to cope or change.

CHAPTER 9

Psychology of Pregnancy: The First Trimester

IF YOU RESEMBLE MOST COUPLES, YOU AP-
proach living pregnant with questions and emotional needs.
Whether this is a first or later child, you wonder:

1. What is happening to me, us, as a couple or family?
2. How can we help ourselves through these months,
the birth, the postpartum period?
3. How easily can we fit the new child into our home
and work lives?

Although everyone must evolve individual answers,
there are some emotional and psychological challenges
that remain constant with many couples during this "normal abnormal state."

Despite U.S. passion for the social sciences, the psychological tasks of pregnancy, as distinct from birth, are
not much studied. For the nonpregnant population, interest stops at a few jokes about inept fathers or the culi-
nary cravings of expectant women.

There are good, but not sufficient, reasons for this.
Pregnancy is more a gradual process than a discrete
event. It is formed of evolving and conflicting variables
that render it hard to study. Carrying a child is an individ-

ual experience, therefore uninteresting to sociologists unless they are demographers gathering statistics of its results—new babies and population trends.

Psychologists and psychiatrists show interest in individual cases, but they, like other physicians, are oriented toward diagnosis and treatment of pathology. It's as if pregnancy is too normal a state to intrigue them for research. And women's movement people believe that since more researchers are male than female, they lack interest in the subject because their own bodies will never experience it. In a period of falling birth rate, pregnancy is no "new" topic like wife swapping or bisexuality.

In any case, pregnancy still lacks a Masters and Johnson to research its psychology or group dynamics.

Some people have noted the lack. Dr. Howard Fisher in *Minnesota Medicine* (February, 1974) writes: "Studies of the feelings of pregnant women are rare. Indeed most physicians doing obstetrics avoid dealing with pregnant women's fears and fantasies." He calls pregnancy "the time of greatest pleasure, the time of greatest fear."

In their book *Pregnancy: The Psychological Experience* (Herder, 1971), psychologists Arthur and Libby Colman wrote: "We began to view obstetrical records in a new light. Many pregnancies were described as routine and uncomplicated when the woman became severely depressed afterward. We wondered how that could be."

Is it condescension or boredom that creates this "pooh pooh, my dear" attitude—and the medical records that show it? This paragraph, for example, was written by obstetrician Sheldon Cherry in *Understanding Pregnancy and Childbirth* (Bobbs Merrill, 1973):

> With the knowledge gained through understanding and education, fear of pain and death can be easily dismissed. Superstitions are also easily cast aside if discussed rationally. Most of the ambivalent feelings toward pregnancy can be resolved when dealt with; women should understand that any body changes are only temporary.

This attitude is not unusual in busy professionals who are tempted or forced to treat patients as cases of recurring symptoms rather than as individual human beings. To it, the pregnant woman or couple may respond, "Yes, it would be lovely if one or two such magic conversations abolished problems, but it's nine complicated months of our lives you're glossing over." Pregnancy means growth; birth brings change. And both these processes can bring conflict.

The psychological truth of pregnancy, as with the medical studies quoted in Chapter 1, involves ambivalence in yourselves and others. How your relatives, employers, and friends respond to your announcement of pregnancy is determined by their own feelings about the pregnant body and about what they gauge of your readiness and attitude.

Mary, 40, and her husband Jim, 37, are now parents of two babies under 2 years old. Mary, who lives near Boston, wrote on my questionnaire that she and her husband of only a few months were "delighted" with the first pregnancy. Family and friends were "mostly happy for us, with a few thinking we were out of our minds at our ages, particularly the women with whom I worked." She added, "I resigned after 17 1/2 years in a very interesting and well-paying job and have no regrets—so far!"

Ann, 42 years old, has five children who range in age from 16 to the new baby. Her reaction to a new pregnancy after 9 years: "Shocked. How are we going to manage moneywise? I'm too old." Her husband's reaction was also "shocked," but "we will manage, we always do."

Ann continued, "Our family was thrilled, especially the children. Friends—some were very happy for me; others felt so sorry for me."

Dr. Spock, in *Redbook* (September, 1969), offers some reassurance:

> When you come to think of it, you realize that no woman could have a totally positive attitude toward an event that permanently changes the course of her life as much as any pregnancy does.
>
> Studies have shown that although a majority of women tend to be less and less happy about being pregnant again as they grow older, nevertheless they are apt after the child is born to be more understanding, more tolerant, more successful in managing and happier to be mothering than the younger woman is.

One psychiatrist summarized this by remarking, "Children do not make good parents."

What about all the older women or couples who do feel ready to tackle pregnancy and parenthood?

A new mother, 41 years old: "When you decide to have a baby at this age, there isn't any doubt in your mind that that's what you want to do. There is none of the compulsion of the younger couple who think that, now that they've been married for two years, it's time to start having children."

Marcie Morton, a magazine writer: "I had a baby at 38 because that was the year my husband and I decided we wanted a baby."

Dr. Jennett, director of Reproductive Medicine at a hospital in Phoenix, Arizona, on treating the older woman: "By and large, she has much more come to grips with life and knows what she is about, and knows that life is risk taking."

Is there psychological wisdom in postponing the first baby until many years after marriage?

Mildred Rosen, commissioner of the New York State Labor Relations Board, married at 32 and waited 9 years to have her daughter. "I have had time to fulfill every interest: in my profession, in religious, civic, and women's groups. I have traveled to Europe, so there is nothing my baby is cutting into. All she's doing is making me happy."

Nancy Schraffenberger, a magazine writer whose first baby was born when she was 38, also stresses this connection between maturity and readiness. "I'm glad I did it this way. I traveled, I had lots of adventures, and I got a really good shot at my career while I was in my twenties. When I had the baby, I was mature. I had solved many of my problems, so I didn't have to grow up at the same time I was raising a child."

Susan M. of Maryland wrote me her summary of the process: "Young mothers have more energy; older mothers have more patience. These are the trade-offs for the woman herself."

Here is Dr. Lee Salk on the value of the older woman's embarking on parenthood only after assuring a stable marriage: "She will have a far better chance of finding the right love and nurturing it to maturity. And if she and her husband chose poorly in selecting each other, they will have ample time either to discover their problems and work them out or to end the relationship without the guilt of depriving children of a normal home life."

Over the last 25 years some psychologists have written about pregnancy mostly as a subtopic in researching the effectiveness of Lamaze or other birth preparation to educate and remove fears. By correlating different constellations of variables, they have also tried to predict what kinds of women will experience easy or difficult deliveries.

Some theories are:

1. Pregnancy is primarily a *developmental crisis* similar to puberty or menopause in a woman's life. It presents opportunities both for regression and for growth as one struggles to accept one's new shape and status. Among proponents of this thoery were Dr. E. E. LeMasters in 1957 and Dr. Grete Bibring, also late Fifties.

2. New parenthood involves a *successful adjustment to sociologic models* for culturally correct behavior during pregnancy, birth, and the postpartum period. These models differ among societies. Proponents: Margaret Mead, Dr. Niles Newton, 1962.

The cultural model for meeting pain or crisis in our society, for example, is the "stiff upper lip" and no hysteria, combined with the use of anesthesia. A related ideal is emotional self-reliance or self-sufficiency. We are encouraged at most to depend on one another inside the family but not outside it. Busy men and, increasingly, women shy away from other adults seeking involvement that might prove draining. "I need somebody to depend on, but I can't have anybody but my son and mother depending on me—because I can hardly keep up with their needs" is how a 50-year-old woman phrased this problem.

Many societies have practiced couvade (French, *couver*, "to hatch"), which regulates the conduct, clothing, or diet of the expectant father as well as the mother during pregnancy. The Phillipine Islands provide oft-quoted examples, like the Ifugao people who do not permit the husband to kill or cut anything during his wife's pregnancy. Relatives must even cut wood for him, which he then carries home.

In Binaley, Pangasinan, a province north of Manila,

the father "literally makes a monkey of himself. When his wife's delivery is proving difficult, the *bilot* (midwife) tells him to crawl down the bamboo ladder on his feet and hands, head first." Such customs may seem quaint or ridiculous until you realize their vital purpose—that the father recognize the pregnant woman and coming child as his own and publicly accept his new responsibility.

Indeed, our society probably suffers from the lack of a similar "rite of passage" for expectant or new fathers. As Alice says, "A woman has her body helping her do that task of orientation. A father has to do it all in his head." American fathers escape both the notice and the praise or consideration that can accompany pregnancy. Childbirth classes with father participation are helping alleviate this problem.

3. Pregnant women or couples can be divided into certain "ideal types" and classified according to *sets of psychological or personality variables.* Particular variables studied have been: (a) maturity or lack of it—Dr. E. Pavenstedt, 1964; (b) amount of negativity toward child-bearing, pain, medical experiences—Dr. Leon Chertok in *Motherhood and Personality,* 1966; (c) pregnancy and birth as peak, even orgasmic, experiences—Dr. Deborah Tanzer, *Why Natural Childbirth?,* 1972; (d) ego strength, nurturance, self acceptance. These factors of a woman's current personality are more crucial than her past history—Dr. Elaine R. Grimm, 1966; Pauline Shereshefsky and Leon Yarrow, *Psychological Aspects of a First Pregnancy,* 1973.

Pregnant or not, if you are interested in the sheer range of human emotion, these studies are fascinating reading. General agreement on what constitutes "successful pregnancy" stresses these areas:

1. A positive reason, or at least readiness for, this particular pregnancy. The baby need not be planned; once conceived, however, it is wanted. Dr. Aubrey Milunsky comments: "In our experience only about 20 percent of women over 35 planned their pregnancies."

Examples of less healthy reasons are: to cement a failing marriage; to obey social pressure from relatives or friends; to cure a sense of personal or career failure.

2. Reasonable mental and physical health.

3. A good or adequate marriage or partner relationship.

After interviewing many women, Dr. Howard Fisher, in *Minnesota Medicine* (February, 1974), wrote:

> The only adaptive use of pregnancy seemed to be within a stable marriage, allowing the woman to make a "gift" of the baby to her husband, simultaneously satisfying her sense of femininity and her husband's sense of masculinity. Once accomplished, strong reassurances to the self occurred, producing a profound sense of security in the woman.

Whatever effect this philosophy may have in hardening sex roles, it does communicate the mystery of mutual giving-receiving-giving that is the heart of satisfying or healthy relationships.

"A LITTLE BIT PREGNANT"

The major psychological task of the nine months of pregnancy is to incorporate the child into one's planning, feeling, and lifestyle. It is a similar challenge for both men and women. For a much desired child, the job is easier, although not simple. Such a woman or couple welcomes their altered self-image(s) as a dream or goal realized. One of my friends, Judy, said, "Both times when we wanted a child, I left out the diaphragm, and that was it. I thought pregnant, I felt pregnant, I was pregnant."

For a woman with irregular menstrual periods or an older woman who wonders whether a skipped period signals pregnancy or the beginning of menopause, these are weeks of doubt, confusion, annoyance. Some women report doctors overeager to pronounce them pregnant, while others suffer the opposite. One told me she was 4 months pregnant before her doctor, despite tests, would admit it. Her cervix "wasn't the right color." Such experiences demonstrate the need for obstetricians to evaluate women as whole beings and not as "detached uteri hanging in the wind." The *best* scientific procedure evaluates all symptoms and factors, and does not fixate on one that must, or must not, be present.

While an older woman may be emotionally ready for pregnancy, she, like her husband, may not have the kind of work she can or wants to drop for an extended period. Happy assimilation of the new pregnancy means locating reliable support services—paid maternity leave, good insurance plan, day-care or a flexible work-time arrangement between spouses.

Dealing realistically with anxieties, new or old, is the next step. "When you lack information, you live in fantasyland" is one mother's comment on educating or re-educating yourself.

Worry and fear are neither neurotic nor abnormal. These emotions have an honorable history rooted in biologic common sense. Without them no animals or humans could have survived.

You can expect such feelings to emerge during pregnancy as a response to your altering body, moods, or marriage. For both sexes, these first months are a time of introspection, ambivalence, re-evaluation of yourselves, your skills, your own parents. To get your emotions under control (which usually means living through them, not escaping them), talking them out in a women's or men's group is very helpful—if this style is appealing or available to you. "Country people have friends; city people have groups!" is one suburbanite's sardonic comment on this process. But it's friends who make groups.

Writing emotions in a diary or journal is helpful. A complete, structured method for this has been developed by a psychologist, Dr. Ira Progoff of Dialogue House, New York City. (See Appendix IV for further information.) His recommended journal has several sections; four key ones are Dialogues with Persons, with Events, with Works, with the Body. The method also honors dreams and fantasies for their teaching or healing power. Dr. Progoff conducts workshops around the country and has written a book to aid individual use of the journal. The method is oriented toward constructive use of one's feelings. You need not be a writer to try it. Dr. Progoff says writers may even do worse at it than other people. "They can worry too much about style or grammar." He knows that the method appeals especially to people at transition points in their lives.

Given the pressures of the modern world, it is fair to assume that most people who begin to use the journal do so because there is a problem in their life that urgently needs to be resolved, an intense and difficult transition through which their life must pass, or a critical decision they must make. Because of the self-balancing process that underlies it, the Journal Feedback procedures facilitate the solving of problems and the making of decisions. The emphasis is on individual growth rather than group participation.

Another useful method, also writing based, is the Marriage Encounter program, which organizes weekends in cities, at campuses, and meeting centers. It combines individual development with group dynamics and a family focus.

MOODS AND DEPENDENCIES—HOW TO COPE

There is sufficient biologic reason for the mood changes many pregnant women experience. Progesterone, the hormone of pregnancy, is a depressant. In particular, the corionic gonadotropin, produced in the placenta during the first three months, causes the fatigue, nausea, and sleepiness some women feel in these early months. Progesterone and a pregnancy-altered level of cortisol (one of the hormones secreted by the adrenal gland) also affect brain activity. They alter the functioning of catecholamines, the chemical substances that control transmission of nerve impulses from one cell to another. Research shows that pregnant women do less well at tests, mazes, puzzles involving memory or muscular coordination, compared with control-group women or with their own performance before pregnancy.

Writing on the complications of pregnancy, Dr. Mark J. Popp concluded, "Feelings of depression in the early stages of pregnancy are very common. In one study 60 percent of the women questioned admitted to some kind of depression. However, there is reason to suspect that the true incidence is closer to 100 percent."

During pregnancy some women resent having all their opinions, needs, or feelings reduced to, or overjustified by, hormones. Others appreciate the extra favors—help with doors or grocery bags, relaxing of customary rules. One friend, several months pregnant and enmeshed in her Ph.D. thesis, was allowed to keep 25 library books overdue because she told the librarian she couldn't carry heavy items across the city anymore.

Included in mood balancing is another task of pregnancy—facing or resolving emotional dependencies. The myth claims that a pregnant woman is more dependent, clinging, childlike, etc., and that this is her husband's cue to become more masculine, supportive (the shoulder to cry on), secure. The reality, especially for older couples, can be different.

Sometimes a pregnant woman has supportive friends or relatives to whom she turns easily. One of my interviewees, an unmarried mother in her late thirties, said, "I grew up with much love. I have love to give. And I have very good women friends. They were marvelous to me." One of these friends accompanied her to her first medical exam, where she went hoping and suspecting she was pregnant, and shared the excitement with her.

An older man or woman may still have a parent willing or able to listen and advise. However, by the age of 35 most people are no longer dependent on their parents for money, guidance, or companionship. If your parents are ill or widowed, they may depend on you for what you might have gained from them at a younger age. "I'd *like* to depend more on my parents," one woman told me, "but, my God, they're always sick and everything upsets my mother. Now that she's retired, her world is so small. She can't deal with anything, let alone my problems."

This is frustrated dependency that, with luck, changes into the middle-aged realization that your parents did the best they could, and no matter what their shortcomings, you have to live your own life. After studying her 65 couples, Pauline Shereshefsky wrote, "The more mature woman tended to define herself in the ways in which she wanted to be like, and those in which she wanted to be unlike, her own mother."

If your parents did not give gladly, and you suffered during your own period of dependence, you probably have trouble now with both depending on others and accepting their dependence on you. Accepting or at least understanding your own process of mental and physical growth, with its inevitable needs, can be your first step toward accepting or reaccepting it in your new child—or in your spouse.

Dr. Grete Bibring, in *Psychoanalytic Study of the Child* yearbook (1961), wrote a sensible explanation of this process:

> Mature dependence assumes differentiation from the object. . . . It also recognizes limits on the part of the giver and does not demand total gratification or total removal of discomforts. Mature dependence means being able to accept what help is available, not rejecting it because it is less than absolute.

LATER BABIES, LATER MARRIAGES

People assume that a second or later pregnancy must be easier than the first because the woman is experienced, or the couple now knows the parenting basics. Yet second-time parents may be especially lonely because less fuss is made over them. They do not receive the pampering interest offered to first timers. With a previous child or children to care for, they have even less time, money, or energy for their own needs.

If there has been a gap of several years between your last and this new pregnancy so everybody had assumed your family was complete, you may be reluctant to announce the impending event. This is when you need the ego strength to ignore the raised eyebrow, the "Why?"

"I guess when the first child comes at 35, they assume it will be the only one," a New Jersey mother of two wrote me. One woman from Long Island, the mother of three sons, told me that her new pregnancy was occurring 17 years after the last. Not the least important reason for this new baby is a new marriage. A 41-year-old woman named Kate, for example, had an 18-year-old son, born neurologically handicapped during her first marriage. When her second husband wanted children, she dared to try again. "If Bill hadn't wanted a child so much, I might have given up the whole idea. The truth is, though, I knew that even if we *did* have a handicapped child, I could handle it. After all, I did it before. And that time I didn't have the help of a loving and supporting husband."

Doctors assume that when a woman accepts such a pregnancy after many years, she wants to feel youthful (which can mean "needed") again. Dr. Spock says: "I suspect there are a million grandmothers in America who'd gladly take another baby, despite great inconvenience, if nature would provide a way."

If you and your spouse accept your late pregnancy with joy, you are blessed and can expect minimum difficulty, physical or mental. If, however, you are already lost in a thicket of qualms, you are not alone among women or men. Dr. Elaine R. Grimm, psychotherapist, in "Women's Attitudes and Reactions to Childbearing," *Modern Woman, Her Psychology and Sexuality* (Goldman and Milman, Charles Thomas, 1969), writes: "The first-year obstetrician learns soon enough that he can't simply happily announce to the woman that she is pregnant and expect her to react with the feeling that she is fulfilling her destiny." The last part of this century is a time when such stereotypes ("women are . . ." and "men are . . .") have finally begun to crumble.

Your ambivalence—"guarded delight" as one couple phrased it—is a normal part of your growth as people and parents in a complicated world.

CHAPTER **10**

Psychology of Pregnancy: Second and Third Trimesters

YOUR SECOND TRIMESTER (4 TO 6 MONTHS) will probably be a pleasant, optimistic time. Morning sickness is past, weight gain remains moderate, sexual relations are possible and desired. During pregnancy, vaginal lubrication and increased blood flow to a woman's pelvis augment desire. Masters and Johnson report: "80 percent of women described significant improvement in sexual relations over the first trimester and over prepregnant levels also."

According to British birth educator Sheila Kitzinger, some women never experience orgasm until pregnancy or the intense sexual opening and awakening that giving birth can be. Midwife Norman Casserley corroborates this.

Some answers I received on my questionnaire to "Happiness in pregnancy is————":

". . . feeling life and sharing it with your husband."

". . . the baby moving."

". . . looking forward to having a baby."

". . . satisfaction, contentment, feeling of purpose."

". . . a happy family environment."

The Tacoma, Washington, mother of four who had her last baby at 40 wrote me, "Except for a varicose vein problem, I usually enjoyed my pregnancies after the first three months and morning sickness were gone."

Of pregnancy as a peak experience, here is a comparison by Arthur and Libby Colman of the first with the second trimester:

> The overwhelming sense is that of ecstasy; the excitement of carrying an invisible fetus in the first trimester is as intense and romantic as falling in love. It brings the same bursts of joy, the desire to sing and skip down the street, the same feeling of being more special than anybody else in the world. If that happiness starts to fade, it is renewed by the baby's first movements, for now the woman has a chance to fall in love with her state all over again.

And one of my respondents wrote simply, "I felt *great* during pregnancy, alive."

The psychological task of these middle months begins with the advent of quickening when you and then your husband can feel the child moving. During the first trimester you both endeavored to include the new pregnancy within your "life frame." Your psychological effort of the middle trimester involves a different, even opposite, task. Having incorporated the child into your body, mind, and lifestyle, you must now begin the process of *differentiation:* While remaining attached to you, the child grows increasingly distinct as it enlarges the womb and pushes toward the final separation of birth. In one parent's words, the baby "seems more human now." Mothers and fathers "begin to talk to it—him?—and wonder what he does all day floating upside down in there."

Generally these months bring a mixture of excitement, acceptance, contentment. If you are among the couples who request amniocentesis to determine whether the baby is free of certain genetic or biochemical defects, the waiting period for test results will span your fourth to fifth months—and bring some impatience or anxiety.

DECIDING WHAT YOU NEED

Suppose, however, you do not feel well mentally or physically. You wonder where to turn. In cities the variety of counseling available is bewildering or at least hard to evaluate.

According to Shereshefsky, the most successful counseling process for pregnant women or couples involves what is called "anticipatory guidance." The counselor neither makes decisions for you nor cons you into "adjusting" to some horrendous reality but supports and listens while you decide what you want to do, how to summon your own defensive strengths. A priest said to me, "Most people are pretty smart. They know *what* they should do. It's figuring out how to do it, grabbing the will power, that bothers them."

It is hard for some couples to experience pregnancy without either wreathing it in illusion or cloaking it in fear. Thus, it is hard, also, for their babies to arrive as individuals instead of as anticlimaxes.

Anticipatory guidance points out, without arrogance, what a couple can realistically expect in each other and in adjusting to new infant care. Whatever the ages of the people involved, such guidance-with-kindness seems a parental function that does help pregnant, questioning couples. Shereshefsky contrasts it with two other approaches that don't succeed as well. One is interpretation, which aims at "major reorganization of the personality" through uncovering conflicts. The other is clarification, which combines "a supportive relationship focused on feeling and stresses" with some counseling on other family problems. The more modest goal of anticipatory guidance —"psychological preparation for the stresses of pregnancy, delivery, and parenthood"—succeeded best in her study. However, all counseled women, regardless of method, "went through the labor and delivery experience with better adaptation than those in the control group."

Since only women were counseled, Shereshefsky's group did not benefit directly as couples from this process. What helped them was the later husband-wife dialogues and emotional openness they engendered.

A comparison of the level of marital adjustment at six months postpartum and at the beginning of pregnancy (first trimester) showed that the marital relationship of the non-counseled group had significantly deteriorated, while the counseled group was found to have held to the initial level. . . . It was our impression from these sessions that the counseled women were more content in the role of mother. They were clearly more open in acknowledging and discussing emotional reactions and psychological needs.

Pregnancy is probably also a good period for marriage counseling by whatever method will build more support or sharing:

Possibly the most burdensome and most pervasively disruptive stress was the circumstance of marital disharmony because of its portent for the future of the newborn infant as well as because of its effect in diverting energies of husband and wife at a time when support from the spouse might have been most needed and appropriate. The one-fifth of couples who were already involved in serious marital disharmony at the time of the first pregnancy disclosed this drain on psychological resources that occurred in the conflict over the marriage.

Birth educators like Dr. Pierre Vellay in France have reported that certain groups of women are particularly hard to prepare or reprepare for easy delivery. Among these are doctors' wives, nurses, women with a history of difficult delivery and/or menstrual pain, women who lost a first child. A nurse said to me, "Well, sure, as a nurse you learn all the statistics and see all the mistakes."

If you have such a fear, however engendered, of hospitals, drugs, or surgery, you no doubt wish the progesterone of pregnancy could bring you amnesia or oblivion. "I'm a large coward," one woman told me; she did not want to participate in the births of either of her children. Dr. Howard Berk told me that about 50 percent of his patients currently request natural (prepared) childbirth; 50 percent do not.

Acknowledge your ambivalence or fears—and *use them* to secure extra help before the Lamaze or other classes begin around your seventh month. One kind of psychological help I discovered can begin in early pregnancy. This is hypnosis, which involves neither sleep nor unconsciousness but a form of guided self-suggestion and relaxation. It has proved effective in removing anxieties, such as fear of heights or flying, in otherwise normal adults and in breaking habits like smoking or overeating.

Lynne Gordon, hypnotherapist and executive director of the Hypnosis Center, New York City, has prepared many women and some expectant fathers for childbirth. One of her patients was Mrs. D., a 34-year-old woman pregnant with her second child; she suffered from obesity and extreme high blood pressure. She wrote Lynn Gordon: "I was tense and apprehensive when I first came to you. The distasteful memory of my previous delivery nine years ago filled me with misgivings about this delivery. After a few hypnotic sessions under your direction I found myself completely relaxed and eagerly looking forward to the delivery."

X-rays at 7 to 9 months showed Mrs. D.'s baby in abnormal breech position, which required extra calming and maternal support. A Caesarean was predicted, although at the last moment the baby turned into normal position, as had been suggested by Lynne Gordon during hypnotic sessions.

"When I first came to you I had high blood pressure of 180 over 150. The doctor I had during the beginning of my pregnancy told me he would probably perform a Caesarean because of my pressure. After going to you, my pressure dropped to a normal 130 over 75 and during the hard labor, the nurse was amazed to find it was 112. She remarked that she had never seen anyone that calm during labor.

"Since I was anxious to eliminate the necessity of receiving the pain-suppressing drugs, etc., used in the hospital, you and I concentrated our efforts to eliminate the pain without the use of drugs. . . . Most women have hard labor from 2 to 3 hours or longer until the actual delivery. Mine lasted about 20 minutes and was actually enjoyable, thanks to your help."

And from Mrs. D.'s doctor, a Manhattan gynecologist-obstetrician with 32 years' experience:

"After 6 weeks of prenatal care I delivered a patient of a healthy baby by natural childbirth. . . . Her desire to want natural childbirth was caused by fears concerning drugs and other traumatic experiences during her previous childbirth.

"I am happy to say that after the conditioning and self-hypnosis taught by Miss Gordon my patient had a completely successful natural childbirth. She was unusually relaxed and thoroughly enjoyed the experience. She was completely devoid of any mental trauma before, during, or after childbirth."

To locate a hypnotherapist or other professional, especially one with medical training, and determine whether you are a good subject for this method, see the address list on page 213. Chapter 16 on birth methods contains a fuller description of how hypnosis operates.

A DREAM IS A DREAM IS A . . .

The dreams and fantasies of pregnant women, as contrasted with "nonpregnant dreams," are one area that has been researched. To summarize the results: From the dream world, there is no good news tonight. Misfortune, harm, and threat to woman or child predominate.

Arthur Colman studied the dreams of 15 normal primigravidae in group sessions and found (1966): (1) repeated nightmares of harm to self or baby; (2) dreams of delivery in which labor was bypassed; (3) dreams in which the mother is excluded and someone else holds the baby.

Robert Gillman wrote on the dreams of 44 pregnant women in Pauline Shereshefsky's book: (1) Forty percent of dreams concerned the baby, compared to 1 percent of such dreams by nonpregnant women; (2) Labor was rarely dreamed, somehow magically bypassed. "All of a sudden I had the baby and wasn't pregnant." The baby was "just there" or already grown beyond infancy.

While the incidence of aggressive acts in these dreams is no greater than the norms of non-pregnant women, the incidence of misfortunes, harm, and environmental threats is high: 40 per cent of the total and over 50 per cent of longer elaborate dreams. . . .

Surprisingly, direct references to orality, such as

eating or drinking, occur in only 4 per cent of the dreams, and references to talking or singing in 16 per cent, a total less than the non-pregnant norms. Regression in time, to a former period of the dreamer's life, is rare, occurring in only 5 per cent. . . .

The group of new mothers that make the poorest adaptation to childbirth, those who suffer postpartum psychotic reactions, are characterized by depression, hostility, and sado-masochistic fantasies. . . . In general, a dream is scored for masochism when the dreamer is explicitly represented as undergoing unpleasant effects or experiences. For example, "I had a helpless feeling. I was trying to reach someone but couldn't. It's a barrier dream. I felt frustrated and unhappy trying to get somewhere but couldn't quite do it."

A typical example is this dream recorded by the American journalist of the Thirties and Forties, Dorothy Thompson. Married to writer Sinclair Lewis, she was 36 and expecting her first child, Michael. The Lewises owned a farm in Vermont, and Dorothy often traveled by train on lecture tours.

I feel very wobbly. Not actually sick but as though I might be at any moment. Last night I dreamed I was on the farm and was driving a wagon load of beans into town down a hill. When I got to the bottom of the hill, I found that the descent had jolted them all out of the wagon and I was terribly dismayed. This is a swell symbolic dream because when I awoke I could explain it immediately. The night before, in the sleeping car, the train had jolted so that I feared it would bring on a miscarriage.

Three years later another pregnancy did miscarry.

The bizarre power and color of such dreams may upset you, no matter what your lifestyle or conscious knowledge that you have no intention of harming yourself or your unborn child. The dreams are more evidence that pregnancy and birth are not only a physical experience. They are, in Chertok's phrase, "a psychosomatic act par excellence."

Pregnancy is an altered state of consciousness. Such

dreams or fantasies are the helpless, childlike or pessimistic, even enraged part of your own psyche aroused by ambivalence or fear. Robert Gillman found this dreaming correlated inversely with a woman's ego strength: The stronger you are or feel, the less likely you are to suffer with them.

Those women who were judged most adequate in adapting to their current life situation, those judged most able to meet their own needs, including pleasure, and those judged to have adequate superegos, had significantly fewer masochistic elements in their dreams.

Whatever reciprocal effect pregnancy and dreams have, dreams by themselves (as distinct from depression or waking masochistic fantasies) are not predictive of maternal adaptation. Gillman writes: ". . . we can conclude that masochistic and hostile elements in the dreams of pregnant women are not predictive of adaptation to the maternal role."

Dreams and fantasies of fathers are even less studied; men may admit them less readily.

Fear for the child was more often expressed postnatally; husbands would admit, once it was safe, that they had worried about deformity or retardation during pregnancy. . . . Almost all the fathers expressed anxiety about getting their wives to the hospital. Many made dry runs. Mr. M. was equipped with flares and emergency equipment should the baby be born in the car.

Psychologists consider a father's *excessive* concern with or for the child as rivalry—fear that the baby will displace the husband in the wife's efforts and affection. Excessive concern would be morbid worry, for instance, about abnormality, neglect, or danger to the baby.

In a group meeting Mr. X. confesses a fear that permeates the entire group. "At the very beginning I would worry about whether the child would survive or not. There was no physical ground for this; there was nothing wrong with the child. . . . The fear that I had most was that he might choke."

"I have that fear," responds another father. "It's not very strong, but I've had it all along, ever since the baby was born." "It is interesting," notes Mr. Y., "that all of us here have had the fear of choking. That's one of the things I'm really afraid of, is that kid choking to death."

APPROACHING BIRTH DAY

Many obstetricians report that the eighth month or the days just before delivery are almost as difficult a time as early pregnancy. Psychologists Arthur and Libby Colman write:

The eighth month may actually be the most uncomfortable time of pregnancy, for then the baby has reached almost its maximum size but has not yet settled down into the pelvis ready to be delivered. . . . In the last trimester a woman's body image is almost discontinuous with her usual physical state. Even for the multipara, the abdomen may seem to swell beyond her previous memories. One primipara said she spent hours in front of the mirror staring at her profile in stark disbelief. At some point, most women will suspect they are carrying twins—how else account for the bulk and the amount of activity in the uterus?

These are the days when a woman is most dependent on others for lifting, carrying, climbing, reaching, and cheering up to fight effects of everything from insomnia to difficulty with bladder control. However, if you've chosen your prenatal care, classes, or other education wisely and can depend on some home support, you'll approach the big day secure, as with other "final exams," that you've done all you can. The next move is up to somebody you already know well—your baby!

CHAPTER 11

Postpartum Period:
" . . . Happily Afterward"

ANN IS A LONG ISLAND MOTHER OF FIVE CHIL-
dren, including three teen-agers. She wrote me that fitting
the new baby, born when she was 42, into the previous
structure of her marriage-family-work life was "absolutely no problem. I've never had so much help." A
supportive home situation, combined with years of experience, builds confidence and optimism. "My baby is a pure
joy—a very happy, healthy baby," Ann continued. "The
older woman can cope easier with problems."

About 30 percent of new mothers, however, experience
postpartum depression for days or weeks. There's some
solace in the realization that the emotional confusion of
this period—blended joy, relief, fatigue—is again a state
you can ascribe to hormones or to the sudden withdrawal
of them that occurs after birth. Suppose you are now
home alone getting to know your baby, or you and your
spouse are sharing shifts. You are attempting to regu-
larize breast- or bottle-feeding, greet visitors, recapture
as much as possible of your normal work or social life.

What kind of woman or couple makes it best through
these months?

Here is one opinion by Dr. Edward Waters, who wrote on "Pregnancy and Labor Experience of Elderly Primigravidae" in the *American Journal of Obstetrics and Gynecology* (59:296, 1950). After researching 649 women over 35 in New Jersey, the doctor concluded:

The older patient, in the absence of complications, has neither more nor greater ills in early pregnancy . . . The most disturbing states tend to develop after discharge to her home. If she has married late, the dislocation is less. If childbearing came late in her married life, then the interference with long established routine is notable, and markedly augmented should infant care become complicated.

I expect this is also true of a couple struggling to adjust to a new baby that arrives so many years after the previous one that even child-rearing practices have changed. One daughter, now 35, said, "I was born when my mother was 30 and my sister when she was 40. I got all the discipline, my sister all the permissiveness."

Several of my respondents became pregnant so soon after marriage that fitting the baby into their lives was simpler because "our situation wasn't structured yet."

The two stages—adjustment to pregnancy versus adjustment to baby care—do not correlate in any simple way that a majority of researchers agree on. Current opinion is that the woman who makes much fuss during pregnancy over diet, drugs, or discomforts may adapt better to motherhood because she is adept at getting what she needs from those around her. She prepares herself or her lifestyle carefully enough so that the postpartum period is no shock. Susan M., 36, of Maryland wrote me of her hospital care for her second birth: "If anything, it may have been more casual because they figured I'd speak up if I needed something, that I'm old enough to know my wants and needs."

Doctors do not consider extreme emotional distance and calmness during pregnancy as a sign of health or good adaptation to parenthood. Psychiatrist Richard E. Gordon of Englewood Hospital, New Jersey, wrote in a medical journal article: "The passive woman may deny her pregnancy as long as possible. She does not get upset because she does not face what is happening to her; neither does she prepare herself psychologically for motherhood."

Increasingly, American couples are getting a good start on the postnatal period with hospital experiences that encourage father participation, liberalized visiting hours, rooming in of mothers and infants, training classes in infant care. What psychologists call "the bonding process" among parents, new baby, and brothers and sisters can begin within moments after birth and is encouraged, rather than interrupted, by the best current hospital or medical procedures.

Complete mental breakdown during pregnancy or the postpartum period is rare in both men and women. Postpartum psychosis affects one in 1,000 to 3,000 new mothers. Libby and Arthur Colman say: "The woman with considerable ego deficits is likely to develop symptoms at some point in the postpartum period, with childbirth itself not necessarily the disruptive stress." By one estimate made in Scandinavia in 1968 by Dr. N. Retterstol, 2 percent of male and 7 percent of female mental patients were hospitalized for illness "related to impending or newly established parental role."

In Dr. Howard Berk's opinion, postpartum depression is caused mainly by previous emotional problems or factors that intensify during the stresses of pregnancy. "It's as if a woman has worn out all her inner strengths and defenses just getting through pregnancy and birth. For the postpartum she may have nothing left."

Any breakdown, other than a mild depression in a woman who was previously coping, signals the need to examine the prenatal or birth care received. How humane —or how disorienting—was it? Were drugs used that can be mood altering, even hallucinogenic (codeine, scopolamine) or nausea producing (Demerol) for some women? It is your physician's responsibility to provide whatever comfort or pain relief you need, but this requires careful consultation to avoid specific allergic reactions to certain drugs.

If you find infant care demanding or if the ambivalence of early pregnancy has reappeared, you will be interested in these comments by pediatrician Lee Salk on his parenting classes: "It is not uncommon for a mother to get a strong sense of wanting to reject her child within a few days after her baby is born. She finds herself thinking, 'He is ugly. How did I get myself into this? I think

I would like to get dressed, leave the hospital, not tell anybody where I'm going, and never be heard from again.' Such rejection is followed by guilt, but the net result is good: the baby gets extra cuddling. . . . In my classes with new mothers, I find that at least one-half of them acknowledge—if only with smiles—that they have experienced these feelings."

And new fathers have similar problems. Dr. George Schaefer, an obstetrician at New York Lying-in Hospital, sympathizes.

You will occasionally have moments when you'll feel that you made a mistake starting the entire thing. You will not be at all unusual—many new fathers have such feelings. The little bit of humanity that is the cause of all your troubles offers few satisfactions to compensate for the many ways in which he has disrupted your existence. The baby does not recognize you, does not smile at you, sometimes seems to scream in fear when you approach, does not do a thing to justify his presence except eat, cry, and sleep —mostly sleep.

Dr. Schaefer's final advice: "Just keep calm during those few weeks—parents always live through them."

KEEPING IT ALL TOGETHER

Dr. Richard Gordon describes those couples who succeeded in minimizing upset:

The couples put somewhat less emphasis on perfect housekeeping than others. They also had some help in the early weeks, be it from family or a practical nurse. Both husband and wife voluntarily cut down somewhat on outside activites. The couples continued to socialize but willingly did so less often than before they had a baby. They kept in close touch with families and old friends. They either moved before the baby came or decided to stay put for six months or so.

And here are specific suggestions made by Dr. Gordon and Dr. Niles Newton:

1. Make friends with couples more experienced than you with babies and little ones.

2. Don't overload yourself with other tasks during this period.

3. Don't be too concerned with how your home looks.

4. Keep up outside interests but cut down your participation.

5. Arrange for baby sitters in advance.

6. If you've considered moving to larger quarters, postpone this for a while.

7. Don't try to take care of elderly relatives during this period.

To which I would add a number 8, appropriate to the Seventies: Try to divide household tasks between both of you or arrange enough housekeeper or day care so that neither of you gets exhausted or martyred.

This may require real negotiation of previous work schedules if both of you after a month's vacation and/or maternity leave want to continue your work lives. According to Pauline Shereshefsky, 57 mothers in her study received volunteered help with household taks or baby care while the infant was a novelty but such help, especially from fathers, "falls off markedly by three months."

Some U.S. companies have seen the need for adequate day care or revised work schedules and have begun to respond, although they remain a minority. A work plan called "flexitime" is now used by 500 firms. It allows employees to choose when they'll start and quit daily within limits, usually 7 A.M. to 7 P.M. Workers can choose which 7 or 8 hours best fit their lives and notify management ahead of time.

On the basis of experience so far, the system seems to work best for white-collar employees who are not involved in shift work or with machines that must operate certain hours. The system is usually optional, and studies indicate that the majority of employees take advantage of the flexibility.

When Arthur and Libby Colman had analyzed all the factors predictive of success with first pregnancy, birth, and mothering experience, they concluded that the quality of a woman's "human supports, what she can give and receive from the people in her life, seems to override all other considerations."

If you are breast-feeding your baby, this alone requires 1,000 calories a day from your body. If you are upset with infant care or that this baby isn't scheduling itself as easily as the previous one, ask yourself further questions.

1. What do I consider part of the good wife-mother role?
2. Why is it (if it is) all my responsibility?
3. Where do I need help?
4. How can I rearrange things to get the help I need?

If you're a new father, ask honestly:

1. What do I consider part of the good father-husband role?
2. How can I share more and/or encourage the older child (children) to help?
3. Do I *really* need the house as neat, my meals as prompt, hot or whatever as they used to be?
4. If I want to criticize, how can I do it constructively?

EVERY PARENT WAS A FIRST-TIME PARENT

"It's much easier the second time around" is typical advice that is typically frustrating to people struggling to do it right or adequately the *first* time.

If you feel you are cramming into a few months what you were never educated for as a teen-ager or an adult, you are not alone. Joanne, a New Jersey mother of two babies aged one and two, is 37 and her husband 38. She wrote me, "Parenthood is a demanding and complex career for which most of us are given no preparation." Nusia, a realistic mother of twins, wrote from Canada, "The trouble with babies is that they're nonreturnable!" Joan (Chapter 7) says, "Babies, especially the first one, create a revolution in a marriage."

The school system of this country, noting how shaky new parents can feel, has started a coeducational work-study program that combines classes in child development with experience at a day-care or other preschool facility. Since 1971, over 200 high schools have offered this "Exploring Childhood" course, but it is so far only for teen-agers. Its best feature seems to be that participation is open to any student, not just those planning to become teachers.

Nobody is born a parent. It is a role that you must grow into by understanding your own behavior and learning to handle your own needs. If you can do this—which is vital to self-respect and cooperative living—you already have a large gift to offer your child.

Dr. Virginia Pomeranz, a lecturer and author, is also a wise pediatrician. Among her basic advice: If your baby is happy and you and your spouse are happy, you must be doing something right!

As an older couple, you've already experienced some raised eyebrows at your new parental status, perhaps in the doctor's offices, in classes filled with teen-age couples, in maternity fashions you find too young. You've heard, "Oh, is this your grandchild?" as you show the baby photos. Relax and enjoy the attention, if possible. People are curious, but such curiosity is usually well meant. And by sheer age, you will escape some of what annoys new parents in their teens or twenties. Since you are 40 instead of 20, people will hesitate before offering the criticism-cloaked-as-advice that young parents receive. If you hear, "In my day we did . . . or didn't . . . ," you can remind them that their day was, or is, your day, too.

This may be the one area where wrinkles or a few gray hairs form a positive asset. If you look old enough to be somebody's grandparent, how can you possibly be inexperienced?

CHAPTER 12

Fathering

"A wise son makes a glad father."
                    Old Testament
"It is a wise father that knows his own child."
          A Midsummer Night's Dream

IF THE INDIVIDUAL OR GROUP PSYCHOLOGY
of pregnant women remains largely unexplored, that of
pregnant fathers is truly *terra incognita*. At a conference
in the late 1960s, psychologist George Stricker quoted
from a research project on personal and sexual identity
completed by a large group of Washington psychoana-
lysts: "Without due foresight, we had initially focused our
attention almost exclusively on the woman, imagining
that pregnancy had to do primarily with what went on
inside her. But the husband's part was forcibly brought to
our attention with our first cases, and we became more
and more aware of his crucial effect on his wife's well-
being."

Dr. Stricker commented: "That a large group of ana-
lysts should omit the husband while studying pregnancy

is less surprising when one realizes that this entire area is remarkable for the neglect of the husband in considering the reactions of the wife."

As a prospective father, you wonder how to help your wife through the coming months *and* meet your own needs for attention, emotional support, whatever you usually receive from your marriage or living relationship. If your partner is a calm, capable person who easily combines her various roles, you are fortunate. Pregnancy and parenthood should bring you minimal disruption.

"I'm waiting for Women's Lib to catch up with *me*," said one older woman I met at a couples' discussion. Besides mothering her three children and stepmothering her husband's three, she also worked outside the home and—most important—the couple seemed to share a loving, long-term marriage.

Suppose, however, your wife is experiencing problems with this new or first pregnancy and her difficulty is unsettling your emotions. If you and she communicate, you may discover among the first of your mutual emotions some jealousy, particularly during a first pregnancy. If she seems introspective or overeager to share with supportive friends who fuss over her and the coming baby, you may feel neglected. Would you be surprised to learn that she envies *your* uninterrupted facility at life's physical tasks—the little items like buttoning your coat, eating what you want, getting away to work on time? Maybe you even regard pregnancy as pretty effortless compared to nine months spent on some project connected with your job.

Pregnancy can be a time to re-evaluate patterns you as a couple have established to meet each other's needs. For most people, this is a process, mysterious, halting at times but never totally absent from a satisfactory marriage, of receiving back what you give, indicating your needs with sufficient kindness to motivate your spouse to respond in her own way.

This interdependent process is no easy skill. Nor does this country's male tradition facilitate it. Our ideal is the strong, silent loner like Humphrey Bogart or James Bond who combines romance, manipulation, and efficiency with an occasional high-speed car chase.

Matured talent with people is best learned from a parent who knew how to do it, who taught without teaching. Because our society has no "rite of passage" (other than cigar distribution) into fatherhood, a man must devise his own by educating himself, assisting his wife's care, including labor and delivery if desired and feasible, protecting and encouraging his new child. Every person needs to take an active, rather than passive, role in such basic life events. Without the assurance that comes from "Yes, I'm doing something, too" or "We're doing something together," various overcompensations result.

Psychologist James Curtis studied 55 normal expectant fathers; his results appeared in the *U.S. Armed Forces Medical Journal* during the 1950s. He found "the frequent occurrence of psychosomatic symptoms to be the most important distinguishing feature in the psychiatric reaction of the men he studied. They developed complaints which were very similar to the complaints of pregnant women."

In Pauline Shereshefsky's study of 64 normal couples expecting a first child during the 1960s:

Sixty-five per cent of the expectant fathers in our study developed "pregnancy symptoms." There were reports of unusual fatigue in the first trimester of pregnancy as well as gastrointestinal symptoms, nausea, backache, headaches, vomiting, and peptic ulcers. A surprising number of fathers gained weight, from ten to twenty pounds, which they lost shortly after the birth of the child. . . .

Several men who had previously neglected their teeth now made dental appointments. A number of men stopped drinking coffee and began to drink milk. Several stopped smoking, not at their wives' request, but "for the baby."

Toward the end of pregnancy, certain men reported great difficulty in sleeping and general restlessness and anxiety. In several instances the husband took to bed.

We find much concern about body intactness and several auto accidents. A number of men became physically overactive; one husband brought evidence of a new soccer injury to almost every interview. . . .

We noted that many husbands began to work frantically during the second and third trimesters. . . .

Fifty-two per cent of the project husbands were largely unavailable to their wives because of heavy work or class schedules. . . .

The beginning of middle age is a time when habits of personality, marriage, or job have solidified because life is easier when it's neither tense nor intense. Some routines of work or marriage are basic, such as division of effort, different areas of competence, so that no person bears the whole effort alone. Less desirable factors may have solidified, also—lack of novelty, boredom, failure, nagging.

If such problems have crept into your relationship, pregnancy can be a welcome, although challenging, time to reacquaint yourself with your partner, who now appears in a new light. If pregnancy is a choice both of you have accepted, what psychologists call "a new alliance" or emotionally expanded marriage should become possible. Here is a description by Arthur and Libby Colman, who have studied first pregnancies and are raising three children. They stress beginning the process early.

If there is to be a mutual alliance, it must begin to be forged at this stage before the uniqueness of their [male or female] experience creates obstacles too great to be bridged.

This alliance cannot simply be a series of financial discussions meant to ascertain new needs of the family. . . . It is, most of all, an emotional alliance, an agreement to be sensitive to one another's needs, to communicate what is needed *now* for one another, to share experiences, to help one another cope with the unfamiliar, the frightening. It must be an alliance to allow growth in each individual, in the couple, growth enough to support the infant they will both care for in the future.

To be a caring human being is an obvious good in itself. It is also, not incidentally, one of the best preparations for parenthood. Sometimes this process does not require so much learning of formal—or manipulative—skills with people as it does responding to what is already working inside you.

An artist and art teacher told me once that participating with his wife at their first son's birth was an energizing experience, a call "to *do* something with my work and our life" that he never forgot.

You needn't be older to feel proud or protective of another human being—but it helps. Dr. Lee Salk even describes what he calls a "fathering instinct":

> I am convinced that there is as much of a "fathering instinct" as there is a "mothering instinct," and I believe men are as protective of their children as women, in many instances more so. I speak not only from professional experience with thousands of parents but on the basis of personal experience as well. . . . Fatherhood does involve hard work, great responsibility, considerable amounts of time, but it also provides untold quantities of joy, satisfaction, and happiness.

Dr. Howard Berk believes that Lamaze or other birth classes help fathers "as much as, or more than, mothers. A father needs to become secure and emotionally involved with his coming baby. How can he do this when he experiences personally none of the growth or sensations? Fathers *need* Lamaze more than mothers."

During the months of pregnancy and after the birth your wife will depend on you for support or courage if she feels alone or isn't receiving these gifts from others. You do your best, but if you find yourself tempted to evade or minimize her requests, problems, needs, worries, re-evaluate how you do feel. Try to supply what seems reasonable in listening, sympathizing, encouraging—and expect that tomorrow or next week, when you need similar support, she will notice and return your gift. Once she accepted you as her husband/lover. Now she is reaccepting you as the father of a child whom both of you have made.

To some men, Women's Liberation is a ridiculous or dreaded concept implying, at least, domestic strife and, at most, the downfall of Western civilization. It's easy to blame women—mother or wife—for personal or familial unhappiness because "family problems are her job, aren't they?" Here's another opinion by Dr. Salk:

> Strange as it may sound, it was not the women's movement that most weakened the family and in the

process taught women to seek satisfaction away from their homes; it was industry and government. I cannot tell you how many cases involving children with emotional problems include mothers who were overwhelmed by having to rear their children alone because fathers were forced to be away. . . . Actually it was not just the stress of the actual uprooting or the periodic estrangement of the father from his wife and children that eroded the family. Rather, it was the overall attitude that everything else was more important than the family.

To date, little has been done to provide flexible working hours for parents of children under the age of three; little effort has been made to accept family needs as being at least as important as the needs of industry or government; and little effort has been made to produce the kind of a parent education that is necessary . . . for the enormous responsibility of bringing another human being into this world.

Mark Feigen Fasteau is a lawyer. He and his wife Brenda, also a lawyer, are parents of a young child. His book, *The Male Machine,* investigates images of American men as they appear in films and TV, sports, government, industry, the military. He is honest about the effect of these stereotypes on the beginning of his own marriage. Whenever he and Brenda had problems, he found himself ashamed and astonished that his emotions proved so strong and that he had such difficulty verbalizing them —if he and Brenda were to talk at all—and choosing words to heal, rather than aggravate, the situation. By contrast, Brenda seemed too verbal, emotional. Here he describes their early efforts at helping each other:

If something upset me, for example, I would often refuse to talk about it. I would agree—after it became obvious anyway—that I was upset and would make to myself, and if forced to Brenda, an intellectualized and summary explanation of what was going on. For example, if I had had some dealings with a professor at law school and had felt less at ease and assertive than I thought I should, I would make an explanation about authority figures and Oedipal complex and refuse to discuss it further. . . .

At the risk of being cursed, yelled at, and, once or twice, physically assaulted, Brenda would insist that I articulate fully what I was feeling. When I wouldn't, she sometimes did the job herself. We must have been a strange sight, sitting together at the long tables in the law-school library, whispering furiously to each other, Brenda insisting and me trying to shove her away and bury my head in my books. A surge of anger and relief told me unmistakably when she was on target. What I was most often upset about was not the objective outcome of the incident, which was usually satisfactory, but the fact that I had felt even the slightest bit ill at ease. . . .

Learning to help Brenda was only a little easier. In those days, she found it hard to ask for help. She would give off a few small distress signals and then, if they weren't picked up, she would get angry. . . . Only as I became more sensitive to (and less fearful of) my own feelings was I able to become more sensitive to hers. . . .

When Brenda would get angry as the result of being unhappy over something, my first instinct, especially if I had nothing (or very little) to do with the problem, was to fight back. I would get knots in my stomach and shout, "What the hell are you telling me for? I don't have to put up with this crap," or tell her she was nuts, both of which made matters worse.

The point of this quotation is not another "Can this marriage be saved?" (itself a cliché) but Fasteau's conclusions about the reasons *behind* such a common male-female communication gap.

What most men want, or at least all that many are capable of accepting, is a kind of passive, appreciative sympathy. ("The guy they promoted [instead of you] sounds like a dumb bastard; he probably plays golf with the president.") Active analysis and intervention is harder to take. ("Well, that's a marketing job, isn't it? And that kind of thing has never really been your style. . . ."); it puts the woman, if only temporarily, in the dreaded position of dominance. Of course, many women somehow manage to give

their men both kinds of help without permanently
damaging the male ego, and, despite protestations of
independence, men depend heavily on that support. . . .

In the realm of emotional support, husbands, for
the most part, do not give what they get. First, a
woman is more likely to be open about her feelings,
so a man doesn't have to work at prying them out.
More important, he is less likely to make an effort to
understand her feelings and needs. Such an effort
would require a conscious expenditure of his own
emotional energy, especially if she is upset or confused and her distress is in some way connected to
him. . . . Staying calm and in control is also easier if
one doesn't get involved. If men can offer practical
advice or take some concrete action, they are often
eager to help. Explaining something or using connec-
tions and influence to help a woman fits right into the
masculine role. So does offering a (manly and silent) shoulder to cry on. . . . They try hard and
often successfully not to notice; they say, "It's just
one of her moods," "Women are that way," or "I'll
never understand women . . ."

These are, of course, generalizations that may not describe your marriage or living situation. You may even
have decided your pregnant wife is so overwhelmed
with her own needs that she no longer offers any of the
"appreciative sympathy" or "emotional support" that
Fasteau claims as women's specialty.

Or your wife, for whatever motives, may be competing
with you to see who can be superparent to previous children or the new baby. There is no *automatic* reason that
"mothering instinct" is always preferable to "fathering instinct." Fitzhugh Dodson, a psychiatrist and father of three
children, says, "My clinical experience is that both
mothers and fathers start out equally ignorant about babies and small children. Mothers eventually learn something about them through sheer trial and error." He adds,
"Fathers are not even that lucky." I take this to imply
that while there is no *one* right (or wrong) way to parent,
there remains no substitute for growth in caring, admitting mistakes, making time available among family
members.

After 40,000 interviews, psychologists Anne Steinmann and David Fox, authors of *The Male Dilemma: How to Survive the Sexual Revolution,* found that the average married couple spends "just 27 minutes a week talking with each other." This is about 4 minutes a day. Another figure is that an average father spends 30 *seconds* a day per child in conversation or interaction. No one begins this way in marriage or parenting. It must be from boredom, lost illusion, pressures of work, illness, unsolved problems, that we find ourselves this way.

A wall plaque I saw in a friend's home summarizes the kind of self-reliance that also allows self-giving:

> LOVE REQUIRES SHARING
> SHARING REQUIRES STRUGGLE
> STRUGGLE REQUIRES FAITH
> FAITH REQUIRES LOVE.

Logically, this is circular reasoning. Emotionally, somehow and not only for people already adept, it works.

CHAPTER 13

Single Parenting

THE MUCH-PUBLICIZED "SEXUAL REVOLU-tion" has made one lifestyle more possible and acceptable than ever before. This is the choice by a single person, man or woman, who decides to have, keep, or adopt a baby, not from grim necessity because abortion or marriage is impossible but from freedom or love.

Steve, a 36-year-old teacher and father of an adopted son, expresses the essence of this life. "I haven't met anyone I can see being committed to as a husband. But does this have to mean I can't be a father when that's a commitment I feel very able to fulfill? Maybe I'm simply a person who would make a better parent than I would a husband." Steve and his son Billy live in a grouping of houses and couples in New Hampshire. Two of the women care for the group's six children, while the men and the other women go out to work.

To succeed at single parenting, you need self-knowledge, self-acceptance; psychological readiness; a definite decision to have the child and a commitment to the tasks involved.

You've met these qualities before in this book. They

are what older *married* people need to incorporate a new baby happily into their lives. However, the single parent will need more of a fourth quality: unusual ego strength, including ability to endure some hostility because of your choice.

If you have earned a living for years and could support a child by yourself, you probably are well advanced in such strength. Here is an example of what some older women experience—and an unmarried, unguilty parent will receive an extra dose. Hilda Lindley is book advertising manager for the *New York Times*. I assume she was married for part of the time she describes in this interview with *Publishers Weekly*.

I think working is a great privilege. I had to earn a living and support children but, really, it stretched my mind and my ego. I was lucky to have the opportunity to work for the kind of people I work for. I never missed a day's work if I had pneumonia or took a Wednesday off to play golf as most of my male colleagues did, or took my secretary out for three hours and didn't return. . . .

There are women quite hostile to women working and having children. I used to have babies in my vacation because I couldn't afford to take the time off. I needed the money. It made me so mad that one time I went to the obstetrician, my heart going a mile a minute. "Hilda, you're a fool," he said. "You must have known when you decided to work and have children you were going to make a lot of people angry. Men who wanted your job and women who wanted to have children. If you're going to let these people reach you, you'd better quit working and stay home."

My interviewing for this book showed me that older people who have chosen unmarried parenthood as a goal rather than a tragedy are impressive individuals—apt to be in good health, earning enough, sure of themselves but fearing that without close human ties, such as a child provides, they would miss some essential of human possibility. Their children represent their commitment to humanity, present and future—not a narrow project for their own self-development.

Of two single women desiring children whom I met at a birth conference, Sara, aged 34, had already questioned her doctor:

"My present gynecologist told me that I have a very small benign growth in my uterus and that I might want to start giving thought that the growth or removal of this tumor could impair my chances for having children later on. He said there was no rush, though, and that I was at present in 'prime condition' for having children (this to a question about my age) and would continue to be so for some years. I felt this was very encouraging since I had a lot of fantasies about mongolism, etc., and miscarriages because of my age. I don't know where these came from since my friends have had children in their thirties and are all very positive about it. Perhaps I got these ideas from reading books: I remember an account of Dorothy Parker having a miscarriage at 40 or something. That worried me a lot.

"I've often thought that things were organized wrong, biologically, because I believe as I've grown older, I've become a better person, have fewer problems, am better equipped to care for a child in every way."

What does Sara anticipate parenthood will teach her?

"Learning how to live with the fact of someone's *complete* dependence on me and with the irrational nature of childhood, and later with letting and helping the child become an autonomous person.

"In my childhood I was often treated as though I couldn't know anything because I was just a kid. This has made me aware, perhaps excessively so, of the importance of letting children be their own people, individuals, respecting their rights. The whole 'children's rights' thing is very important to me. Also I think my parents invested too much of their hopes and so forth in me. If I failed or succeeded, it was a reflection on them. I don't want to do that. I don't want to use my children to 'prove' something about myself, and would like to try to treat them as people that I love and have a special relationship with, rather than as 'mine.' "

A woman in newspaper and advertising work wrote me:

"I have been a late bloomer . . . now doing things that I missed years ago. I have been affected positively by the women's movement, feeling comfortable in my single state.

"I approach feminism from an almost mystical point. I believe in the special sensitivities of woman, archetypally, and that the childbearing experience—while not essential for every woman to go through—still is central to female consciousness.

"Accordingly, within five years—married or single—I would like to give birth to a child."

This preconsideration of parenthood as loving, careful choice—rather than something fallen into merely because one is married—is thought provoking because it is rare in our culture, at least among young parents.

Some single people frankly prefer children to adults. Jean, about 45, speaks about her daughter:

"I suppose I've never been the kind of person who really wanted day-to-day intimacy with other adults. I adore being with children, but I really tire rather quickly of other people unless there's a true respect for the other's privacy. The one time I lived with a man I found it very difficult. . . ."

How does she solve this problem in living with her daughter?

"I just tell her I want to be alone for a while and get her something to do. I don't know, maybe it's that she's always lived with my particular lifestyle, but we seem to move to each other's rhythms much more than I'm able to do with other adults."

Laura Hobson is a novelist who chooses sexually controversial themes for her books. Dori, the 40-year-old heroine of her novel *The Tenth Month,* discovers after what used to be called "an affair" that she's pregnant. She decides against abortion; she had wanted a child badly during the years she was married and treated for infertility. "I couldn't possibly conceive, that word—mysterious, powerful, ordinary, gigantic—became I have conceived. I could never conceive, I did not conceive, but now I have conceived. What a conjugation for a woman of 40." Taking a leave of absence from her job, she gets a new apartment, has the baby, and prepares to return to her former life with her "newly adopted" son. She even arranges legal papers to legitimize her choice. This absorbing novel ends, however, with a credibility gap: The gynecologist who has treated her for years has been impressed with her strength; it is hinted that he will marry her!

I talked with one 40-year-old woman, a student and social worker, who had undergone an abortion only two days before we met. She said, "I wanted to have the child. At my age I know it's probably my last chance, but my boy friend didn't and I just couldn't imagine how to do everything—go on in my field, pay for day care, love a child properly all by myself."

One study of unwed mothers (all ages) showed that 6 years after their babies' births, 50 percent had married. Of these, 25 percent had married the child's father.

Bowing to the sexual revolution, social service agencies have eased some of the pressure on unwed mothers to surrender to adoption or abortion. With the coming of day care in cities, some of the guilt over achieving adequate supervision is lifted. Single parents can now blend without shame into the general landscape of "parents without partners," some of them proudly so. Certainly their previous and awful uniqueness, some of the neuroses or attempts to overcompensate, have lifted. "I'd tell any single parent," said one psychologist, "not to worry as much about what their kids are missing and concentrate instead on gaining self-confidence and assuming their own responsibility."

Not everyone has a talent for, or interest in, marriage. Some 8 million U.S. children currently live with one parent or none. Single parenthood is a lifestyle mainly for the sturdy of soul and body, but it is no longer one that needs apology.

CHAPTER **14**

"Life Is What Happens While You're Making Other Plans!"

ALICE, WHO WAS 42 WHEN HER SON WAS born, has experienced parenthood from both worlds— single and married—and several continents. Her decision to continue pregnancy and give birth was a conscious choice, one part of a story filled with loving acceptance of responsibility plus tricks of fate. She spent the final, revealing months of pregnancy "hibernating," communicating only with a few friends around the apartment house where she lives. She and Claude, the baby's father, are now married. They met in a foreign country in which she worked for several years.

A writer and artist, Alice is an energetic woman with tawny, wavy hair. Shortly before our interview she had returned from negotiations in Hollywood to produce an animated film from one of her books. During our talk she nursed her happy, healthy 16-month-old son Marc.

Combined events, such as traveler's abdominal complaints (misdiagnosed by a doctor) and a functioning menstrual cycle, masked Alice's pregnancy for many weeks. Finding yourself not only pregnant but four months pregnant and unmarried in your mother's home town is a challenge no matter how strong your character.

"When I missed my first period, I thought there was a chance of pregnancy. Then my second period came, and I felt assured I wasn't. I did consult a doctor for diarrhea and a vaginal infection, which I'd had before. He didn't examine me. He just prescribed flagyl pills and ordered lab tests for the diarrhea. Later I worried about these pills, knowing some drugs at the wrong time can cause congenital defects. . . .

"I knew it wasn't menopause. In no way is my body functioning at its chronologic age. When I had a complete physical a while ago, the doctor said I had a body like a woman of 30.

"Because I wasn't married and had always lived a very different vocation from raising a child, the pregnancy was problematic. I wanted *not* to be pregnant and hoped it wasn't true. As I read more in *Our Bodies, Our Selves*—this was already at 3 1/2 months—I feared I was. I didn't have any classic symptoms like morning sickness."

I naturally wondered about the father's reaction since he was two continents away. I asked Alice's views on abortion and adoption.

"Neither of us had planned on marriage to each other or to anybody else, nor had either of us foreseen a child in our life frames. At the end of my overseas work we didn't imagine I was pregnant—my second period had come strongly enough to end worry about my first missed one. I flew home on schedule, thinking about this relationship, however.

"Even to get word to Claude was a feat. I had to write a code that only he would understand. He answered with a beautiful letter that he, like me, had mixed reactions. Because we'd talked about the possibility of pregnancy, I knew he wouldn't tell me to have an abortion. Despite uncertainties in our relationship, his reaction was encouraging and heartwarming. A new life under difficult circumstances was not a totally terrible thing for him.

"Well, of course, I considered abortion—for about a day. I thought I *should* think about it since it is a solution for so many couples. Because my second period had come, it wasn't until I'd missed my third that I thought again, Gee, I really *must* be pregnant. The anguish I felt when I missed my first period returned. I couldn't get an appointment with a doctor for a week. I thought,

How awful. Then I was glad I had another week of not knowing whether I must change my life completely.

"I dismissed abortion. Because of my religious upbringing, I believe we can't treat a life like that. However, I don't judge anyone who has an abortion. I understand why people do—the dimensions of anguish—that it would be an easy solution compared to the months and years, the publicness of having the baby that proclaims to all the world what you've been up to!

"If I hadn't believed the father's response would be positive, I might not have told him. Perhaps I'd have had the baby alone and placed it for adoption. It was a long terrible time, yet the planning I had to do provided a clarity."

I asked Alice about her family, especially her mother, who is 65. It was her mother's doctor who finally confirmed the pregnancy.

"I told my mother several weeks after I discovered I was pregnant. That was probably the hardest thing she's ever been told by anybody. It took her several months to recover and begin to deal with the reality.

"It's a tribute to her faith. She came through affirming life and belief in the baby. She has not been bad to the father, accepts him for himself, only hopes he will be good to me. When the baby was born, she stayed some weeks with us. Now that we've been together more, I know she loves the child very much. At first it was traumatic for her, but one of the first signs she was coming around was, 'Alice, you know I've included the baby in my will.' That was very touching, something you don't expect. Her first reaction had been, Don't tell anybody, have the baby—'Maybe you can say you adopted him?' —but don't marry the father.

"She admitted she'd long ago pondered what to do, should this happen to any of her children. She had decided she'd take the child and raise it as her own. 'But now with this happening at *your* age and at *my* age,' she said, 'I can't do it.'

"In many black or Latin families a daughter can return home after a baby or a difficult marriage. That isn't possible at my ripe old age. I did connect my mother with the few friends I had told so that they could comfort her."

Where did Alice turn for assistance? She participated in a consciousness-raising group whose members "helped me so much." The women met for a year and a half, finally disbanding because people moved away.

Through her work she had already made other friends who now offered practical, nonjudgmental help. "Here in these buildings I knew both single people and married couples with children. They noticed what I needed and helped me work through the problems—relationship to the father, the physical, mental, and emotional strains, the medical aspect. Because I remained uncertain about keeping the child, no one offered baby presents before I went to the hospital.

"Then I made my decision to accept him with its consequences. When I came home a week later, people had fixed a complete baby section in my apartment—crib, clothes, blankets, toys, diaper table, a gift of diaper service. All I had to do was lay him in the crib."

She told this simply, but it was a touching moment in her life as such a gift—finding love and care just when you most need them—would be to anyone.

PREPARING FOR DELIVERY

Alice had an active pregnancy. She received some private tutoring in Lamaze exercises beginning about her fifth month from a midwife who also lived in one of the apartments. She feels her daily practice benefited her and aided postbirth recovery.

"I had a relatively easy pregnancy. I do remember being always tired in the beginning. That tired weightiness continued through the hot summer. It makes you appreciate how light and airy you usually feel. Then at six months I made a big trip overseas. I returned to this country at the last moment they allow pregnant women to fly. I didn't want to examine dates too closely. I didn't carry large, and wore loose clothes, like huge serapes, so people even then might not have guessed—if the wind wasn't blowing a certain way.

"During pregnancy you're unusually concerned about yourself and your health. In my dreams, giving birth was easy, but in one I remember my great joy that the baby had only five fingers and five toes on the right places. You feel so responsible for this life you're carrying. Exercises and ordinary activities like driving a stick-shift car or carrying things get harder. You become dependent on others in a whole new way. It's hard to imagine myself pregnant again or with a new baby plus, say, a 2-year-old who constantly needs picking up. But I know many women do it.

"The last two months were the heavy heat of August and September. My feet did swell but not seriously enough for bed. I slept with feet elevated. I did gain 25 pounds.

"When I returned from overseas just before the birth, I was preparing an apartment in the next building, carving out a place for us in the basement, building walls, making a room with some people's help, worrying about when the father could arrive. He did arrive before the birth and stayed as close to me as they let him in the hospital."

I asked about Alice's doctor. The midwife in her building recommended him because she knew he could appreciate difficult circumstances yet not pressure for abortion. Although the birth required major surgery, both the doctor and the hospital midwife, knowing Alice lacked medical insurance and Claude was not employed in this country, donated their services.

"I've given the equivalent money to another cause. I feel that's a beautiful way to live, each helping each. . . . He's a wonderful doctor, originally from a small country near the U.S.S.R. He's worked here for years. Most delightful, zestful man I've ever known. He'll meet you, hug and turn you around, give you a big kiss. His office was a bright spot during pregnancy when I wasn't sure the father and I could meet again or when.

"Some things this doctor said bothered me such as, 'Don't worry about a thing. Just leave everything to me. I'll be responsible for the baby.' I can understand his approach and attempt to allay the fears and worries that bog a woman down. But from reading *Childbirth Without Fear* and other material, I know it's the woman who has the baby, not the doctor. I let him know I didn't want sedatives or any of those things they give to make it easier for them. . . .

"The waters broke, not in a sudden flood, but up high so I was leaking. I went to the hospital. The baby was wedged in breech. The doctor said if I didn't begin labor that night, he would do a Caesarean in the morning. I feel he'd already decided on a Caesarean, however. I did agree to it. I believe it a wise and proper choice because I was quite unsure I could have delivered that baby without one or the other of us getting greatly messed up. To me, that's why you need and should have a doctor available—in case of emergency that no one planned, but there it is.

"The midwife stayed with me throughout the night. She knew I wanted to be as 'into it' as possible. She described spinal anesthesia and asked whether I'd had serious back problems that would preclude its use. Certainly I wanted to be conscious."

Alice described the Caesarean, which took "maybe an hour, although they had the baby out in 10 minutes. The funniest thing happened as I lay on that table. I was so bright and shiny asking all these questions in order to understand what was happening. A nurse told me later that when I asked, 'Are you cutting now?' the doctor was already pulling the baby out! I had felt nothing of his cutting through three or four layers of me. The doctor spent the rest of the time sewing me up. He does a horizontal Caesarean and brags about how you can wear a bikini afterward. However, since I'm not the bikini type, I didn't need that. The baby was normal, 7 pounds, 4 ounces. Beautifully shaped head."

The brand-new father had a surprise, too. "There was no labor in my case, and the actual birth was so fast. He'd just settled down to the long traditional wait in the fathers' room, beginning to read, when the midwife came and informed him he was father to a son. He wasn't prepared at all. He just said, 'Huh?' He couldn't register what she said because he'd been sitting just 10 minutes. . . . Now he loves the baby very much."

Alice recovered well from anesthesia and surgery. "They tell you to lie very still for 12 hours. So I lay still—and didn't get the headache some people get. The next day they get you up to walk, you don't feel like it. For walking, I had a heavy binder over my abdomen. I walked doubled over with pain for three days. However, the pain does recede. It's all bearable. I wanted to get home because I had no insurance. I was paying by the day at the hospital."

Although Alice's care from her doctor and midwife

pleased her, some apparently rigid hospital rules troubled her. She remains sorry that she didn't inform herself or see the head nurse sooner. "I was most concerned about starting breast-feeding. I'd been told I'd get the baby after 12 hours but not told about a special hospital rule that Caesarean patients don't get the baby for 24. They want to observe him in the hours after birth because a Caesarean baby doesn't undergo certain invigorating aspects of normal birth. His mouth and throat may be more clogged with mucus, for instance.

"I made a big fuss about not seeing my son. Finally, the nurses brought him—for five minutes. However, I still wasn't allowed to nurse him for 24 hours. I guess I feared my milk wouldn't come if I didn't start promptly. When you're older, you're not sure how much age will influence anything.

"I wanted to nurse on demand but received my baby only every four hours, just like the bottle babies. He might be sleeping, but I was supposed to nurse. When he cried later—never mind. The last day the head nurse visited. When I expressed grievance at their not supporting the breast-feeding mother by letting her visit the baby or bringing him on demand—it's laziness on their part—she said they should have done so. I had assumed only-every-4-hours was another rule. I should have challenged harder.

"Most women were bottle feeding. I was the only one breast-feeding except for a young black mother who also got up my first nursing night. Every other night I was the only one of about 20. This was a low-income hospital where my midwife-nurse friend works. Despite lack of insurance, it was good I remained there a week and got walking again because I had a strenuous life when I returned home."

How does Alice feel about home delivery? "It would have been my style. I read about it in the *Birth Book* from California [The Birth Center, Santa Cruz, Calif., is a group of lay midwives who do prenatal education and many successful home deliveries.] and other materials. If I'd been younger, I might have. The midwife might have, but even she was oriented toward a hospital. However, my doctor wouldn't have been amenable."

Another of Alice's hospital worries concerned registering the baby when she was not married to his father. The wheels of law, custom, and society turn slowly, but for Alice they had turned just in time. "We were able to register the baby in the father's name right at the hospital because a new state law had been passed a month before. A baby used to be registered in his mother's name and 'unregistering' over to the father's name later required a whole legal procedure. Somebody had brought suit and won; I didn't even know it until I went lugubriously to register on my last day. The clerk said, 'You could have come earlier. Just bring the father along to sign.'

"It means we both acknowledge this child, both wanted him to exist despite uncertainty. This is Claude's first-born son."

Alice's relationship with the father remained uncertain, but some months later they did marry because "he wanted to very much."

BREAST-FEEDING ADVENTURES

Alice emphasized that her protein-balanced diet (Chapter 8) plus exercise plus months of breast-feeding have all kept her trim and healthy. "Now I feel or see no physical effects of pregnancy except for the Caesarean scar." When I visited, she was doing full nursing, four or five times a day. The baby was lively, sliding downstairs on his stomach, walking, saying his first words in two languages.

"I'm glad I don't have to work outside in this society that does not provide nursing mothers with day-care centers on the job. Babies are babies such a short time. I wanted to start him off with this gift of nursing. I had thought before our Hollywood trip at 9 months that I could wean him, but during the trip seemed a bad time. I didn't really *have* to.

"I've read that a woman can get sexual satisfaction from nursing, but I've not experienced that. The tenderness and trust, the warmth, closeness, and giving are more important. I just can't believe a woman wouldn't do it if she could. There's also the school of thought that says let him wean himself when he's ready."

I remarked that just then her full, sleepy baby didn't look at all ready.

"Right! Somebody said to me, 'It's all right, Alice. As long as he's weaned by the time he goes to college.' My mother and relatives breast-fed but stopped at 6 or 9 months. I get cracks about 'Is that baby still nursing?' Here I don't face that pressure; it's much more do-your-own-thing.

"It's acceptable for little babies to nurse, but when a baby is walking, it's less so. I was nursing him on an airplane where a baby needs comforting from hurting ears. The man next to me said, 'I'm *glad* to see you nursing a baby. I don't see that very often.' He said his wife had nursed their two sons for 26 and 27 months and is now nursing a third child. I asked, 'Does that make the child more dependent?' 'No. My boys are 4 and 5 now and doing fine.' It's easy to nurse in public. Most people think the baby in your arms is sleeping."

I asked what kind of clothes Alice wears to achieve this. She favors sweaters, tunics, pants and said she hadn't tried a zippered (back or front) garment for two years.

"A woman I met in Seattle was nursing her child—she knew it would be her only one—and was in her twenty-seventh month. Finally, one day her son said, 'Mom, no more milk. Enough milk.' She said that was it. He never did it again. Maybe there are some natural cut-off points you shouldn't miss."

WORK AND THE OLDER MOTHER

Next Alice and I discussed Marc's impact on her professional life. "Before discovering the pregnancy, I'd just finished a whole project of work with groups, social development. So the baby came at an interim period.

"New creative work in art or literature is beyond me right now, although I still must do my tax returns, letters, see my lawyer, keep up minimal responsibilities. I exchange baby-sitting with people here and take my son with me almost everywhere. People accept it, although it takes me longer to arrive and complete business once I'm there.

"I was away from Marc the first time when he was 7 months old. After the first year I'd been away only three times. That sounds worse than it felt. We experienced many new things together, traveled to foreign cultures, when he was 5 to 7 months. I always wonder what he sees. It's an actual pleasure for me after so much running around in my life to have this quiet time with a young, growing preson.

"In my unmarried life I had many friends and talents but no *clear* idea with whom or at what I should work. Now some central priorities are clear. However, this life is all-demanding. With the baby I seldom have uninterrupted time. The diaper-changing and food-fixing routine usurps hours.

"I worried that I would resent him for occupying my productive time. It does bother me but not as I feared; I've really enjoyed so much having him. My perennial faults, like lack of organization, bother me worse now. They show more because I have this new demand on me for always-availability.

"However, to be present as another human grows— the rate of growth—is so exciting. When he had several naps a day, whenever he awoke was a new day. You can see and feel the changes, especially now that he walks and talks. You think: If only more of us could experience life as he does. He trusts and isn't afraid of anybody so far. I do plan on day care. It will be good for him as he grows."

Alice and I disscussed abilities of older parents. I mentioned that Dr. Spock believed that the older woman, "secure in her maturity," can enjoy the special charms of children more than a younger mother.

Alice laughed. "I don't know whether I'm 'secure in my maturity,' but I have been able to relax and enjoy this baby. I don't weigh the time he takes. That amazes me."

Dr. Virginia Pomeranz is a New York pediatrician whom I had questioned about the older parent at a public talk on child rearing. Her wise viewpoint is that parenting skill is "not a matter of age but of readiness for the tasks." This means that new parents must mature quickly in very opposing ways—first to incorporate the child into themselves and their lives, then gradually to let go.

Alice responded, "I didn't know or read that, but it's certainly true! One of the main jobs of pregnancy, at no matter what age, is to accept the baby. In my case, that was quite a job, but I did it. However, I know I mustn't take too much pleasure in his present dependency but encourage him outward, not pity him too much when he falls and bumps his head—how to help him learn that certain bumps are part of life. I've noticed that when I act as if it hurt, he'll cry; if I don't, he doesn't."

BABIES AND GRACE

At several points in the interview I asked Alice what advice people had given her related to age, and what she was learning from pregnancy and parenting. Her replies were thoughtful, joyful, an affirmation of a common human experience—that when our need is the greatest, the greatest help can come, especially as with Alice, when helpers saw all her efforts, too. She felt it first in her decisions against abortion and adoption when she tasted both the advice that helps and the advice that condemns.

"I came to live with people tolerant of my unmarried state and decision on abortion. I did not tell many others, like my relatives, who would have had much more advice —and did—when I told them the week before the birth. They *definitely* felt I should give the baby for adoption. For them an intact family is essential to raise a child. People here felt I could decide to keep the baby even if I didn't marry the father. I was anguished whether greater love for the child should mean giving it for adoption.

"I remember praying with several people one night. A priest said he felt the Lord wouldn't want me to bear such a problem for the next 20 years of my life. He didn't mention adoption, but that's what he meant. I felt trapped in the question; anxiety is so small a world. I tried a few days living wholeheartedly with that option—and found I couldn't do it. There were no pressing economic or health reasons why I could not adapt to fit the new life—and give up a good night's sleep and much of my career for the coming years.

"But the other side is that I receive so much in return, a great grace. I've never once regretted having or keeping the baby, although life remains tough. I've been unable to return to other work besides struggling with the relationship to my husband.

"To surrender the child would also have been hard, although I believe most adoptive parents are loving people who want a child badly. Another problem is that every adopted child asks about his real parents. Although there may be traumas for Marc from my circumstances, his father's life, our struggle to relate, there is something to knowing who one is, whence one came.

"People were so kind in not pressuring or offering me baby gifts before I'd made up *my* mind. So much then got done for me. That love was so moving. I've learned a lot. I've bought practically nothing because another woman here had a baby boy just three months before me. That money can be available for other needs. I've passed the baby things on to other children."

Alice believes the most important lesson of parenting for her is that life is one continuum. In religious language, this would mean that there are many ways to God. Although you change your road, job, country, the path leads on.

"I felt very close to God during late pregnancy. What I doubted was not relationship to God but to the baby's father. . . . The horror of knowing myself an unmarried mother in the background I came from. Yet to be convinced through some people's beautiful reactions that I was all right before the Lord. I had never experienced that so deeply. It was no churchy time, although I went regularly—rather an abiding sense that the Lord loved me and this child more than I could. That things would be okay, although I didn't *know* whether *anything* would be.

"We know from psychology that parents can put all kinds of spooky things onto children. Such responsibility is spooky. How to trust, play each day as it comes, consider the future but not let it weigh us down."

Finally, she remarked that what she had liked about pregnancy was "to have new life inside me, that what I'd thought would never happen was happening—when I hadn't worked hard for it. To touch that mysterious life we're responsible for, yet is beyond us. . . . In a way, pregnancy isn't long enough—or mine was shorter than most. However, if you don't take time to reflect, you can pass through it oblivious as through other important experiences."

When she said, "Life is what happens to you while you're making other plans. Quotation from one of my friends," I asked, "Do you know its companion piece? 'Love is what happens when two people meet each other and get confused'?"

Alice laughed. "Oh, my husband would like that one."
"If men could get pregnant—?"

"They'd be less casual about that which causes pregnancy."

"And fatherhood is—?"

"Even more difficult than motherhood," Alice concluded. "A woman has her body helping her to do that task of orientation from being one person to two people. A father has to meditate, do it in his head vicariously. He has to accustom himself to responsibility for a child in a whole different way. I felt for the father of my child, was glad he would give this child his name. That seemed the only real act he could perform to acknowledge his new status."

"Motherhood is—?"

"A demanding, joyful thing."

CHAPTER **15**

Labor and Delivery: Your Choice of Methods

IF AS AN OLDER COUPLE, YOU'VE WAITED UN-til now to have your first or later child, you are fortunate in at least one way. The women's movement, aided by various hospital and insurance reformers and certain pioneering physicians, is facilitating one of your largest tasks —to locate the kind of delivery, the combination of features, that best fits your medical and family situation.

None of the methods described in these final chapters is new. Chinese acupuncture, for instance, dates to at least 1000 B.C., midwifery to the origin of the race. Even the controversial decompression equipment is almost 15 years old. Yet all methods, slowly and together, are changing and humanizing the practice of obstetrics in America.

The specific methods I discuss are Lamaze, Read, Dr. Leboyer's birth without violence, Sheila Kitzinger's psychosexual techniques, husband-coached birth, acupuncture, hypnosis, cervical vibrator or dilator, decompression equipment, and delivery by midwives in new "birth homes."

The common criticism you hear about any "new" method is, "It's only a fad," or "It's too dangerous." However, all these methods assume that for an experience to be "safe" does not mean that it need be unconscious, impersonal, tension filled. For many women, these last qualities practically guarantee an unsafe or lonely delivery with the earliest resort to anesthesia or surgery to repair situations proceeding out of control.

My general opinion is that results of all these 10 methods follow what statistics calls the "bell-shaped curve." At each end of the bell for any method are a few people who, using it, judge themselves and are judged to have done either very well or poorly. They are the inevitable extremes and follow the rules of any grading system: Motivated individuals after careful preparation are apt to succeed (however defined). The unmotivated or unconcerned can expect, if not failure, then certainly more surprises, upsets, challenges.

Most people—the average or median—will range in the center for any human variable such as height, weight, I.Q., or skills, including the ability to control labor contractions. This is boring to those who would foster genius (the top extreme), but if most adults were not at least average in competence and adaptability, we would already have followed the dinosaur into extinction.

The bell-shaped curve is the only explanation I can devise for why some people do well with the Lamaze method of prepared birth, for example, while others, who also followed classes and exercises, fail or report, "Well, it helped but not enough for what I needed." Since birth is a psychosomatic event, the problem is also psychological: Eight to 12 weekly classes sometimes cannot repair the stereotypes of a lifetime—that birth is a dangerous, painful event best dozed through or handled by doctors. When I asked one woman whether she wanted to be awake for delivery of her second child, she answered, "No. I'm a large coward." Another told me she didn't want her husband present because "I wouldn't want him to see me in distress if he couldn't help me."

It is true that a woman's body, particularly for second or later births, will tell her when to push, when to relax—if she knows how to interpret the signals. Birthing is a physical skill. Like much simpler examples, such as bicycle riding or swimming, it involves sensitizing oneself to what is happening, the motion, balance, rhythm, and going with it rather than against, or despite, it.

Erna Wright has a famous estimate: "The uterus does 80 percent of the work of pushing a baby out of your body. You do 20 percent."

DOCTORS LAMAZE AND READ

Throughout human history some fortunate women have done birth well by learning it on the spot. One of them educated Dr. Fernand Lamaze in France about 40 years ago. When he noticed her success and joy and asked why it hadn't hurt, she answered, "It wasn't meant to, was it?"

Dr. Frederick Leboyer, also a French obstetrician and originator of "birth without violence," describes his moment of truth—not with a woman but with a laboring goat on a hillside. Just as he was about to move in and apply his years of experience to her condition, he discovered that at most he could only assist her with her own procedure. " 'How can I help you?' was my first thought. Then I realized she didn't need my help, but she was afraid of me. So I sat down and watched, which quieted the mother who saw that I wasn't a dangerous wild animal!"

In the 1930s I. Z. Velvovski and other Russian doctors, basing their work on hypnosis and Pavlov's methods of conditioning reflexes, began the modern movement of natural or prepared childbirth. In 1951 Dr. Fernand Lamaze visited the U.S.S.R. and introduced this "birth without pain" method to Europe. During the Forties Dr. Grantly Dick-Read had already developed his "birth without fear" in Great Britain. The usual armed camps of supporters and detractors assembled—with parents and babies caught somewhere in the midsection. "Natural birthers" had on their side the cunning query flung out by all reform movements to their establishment detractors: "If your methods are fine, why are so many people unhappy with them?" Without either government or party, childbirth became a politicized subject and has remained so.

In 1959 Marjorie Karmel's book, *Thank You, Dr. Lamaze,* plus the work of educators Elisabeth Bing and Erna Wright, introduced prepared birth (also called the "psychoprophylactic method") to the U.S.

In general, the Dick-Read method stresses relaxation as the key to conquering fear, tension, pain while the Lamaze method is a more active training in breathing, massage, and exercise techniques appropriate to each changing stage of labor and delivery.

In 1960 the American edition of *Childbirth Without Pain* by Dr. Pierre Vellay, Dr. Lamaze's associate, appeared. Here are shortened accounts by two older, "high risk" women who achieved happy births despite initial doubts.

Mme. Dietrich was 41 when she had her 6 pound, 15 ounce girl. It was a breech birth; labor and delivery lasted 24 hours.

I was expecting my first baby and I was forty-one years old. It was to be a breech presentation. The child was still in a very high position and a Caesarean was planned if things became complicated.

I regularly attended the lectures on childbirth without pain and was much interested. Each lecture made me discover what childbirth really is. I gradually lost my fear, which had been more or less suggested by my friends on account of my age and the position of the baby....

On a Friday morning she felt the first contractions, not strong or regular, so she postponed going to the clinic until 10:30 Friday night.

... my husband went back home. I felt lonely and a bit nervous. My baby moved a lot and caused strong contractions in the lumbar region. I did not want to cry out because I had to conserve my strength, and I tried to think of the doctor's last words: "What a wonderful achievement to bring a baby into the world.... It is only you who can make a success of your childbirth." In the calm of the clinic I relaxed. It was the beginning of hours of waiting, but I wanted the baby and I was happy.

At 6:30 A.M. the midwife examined me and— pleasant surprise—I heard her say that I was half dilated.... The assistant arrived almost at once, and the presence of this kind, energetic person brought me new comfort and helped me to remain calm....

She massaged me and began the quick respiration with me. She anticipated and guided all my reactions. The contractions were now continuous. . . .

The doctor arrived. I was well relaxed, and we noticed this immediately. For a breech, delivery should be quick. . . . Then he said, "Here are the little buttocks. It's a girl!" I gave a second push. This time I felt my baby coming out of my body—an unforgettable experience.

The doctor put my little Claire on my stomach (eight o'clock).

And Mme. Planadevall, who was 33 when she delivered her first baby, an 8 pound, 10 ounce son:

. . . I should mention my state of mind when pregnancy started. A complete change took place between the beginning of pregnancy and childbirth, a change which greatly surprised my family and friends.

I am abnormally afraid of pain, not only in myself but in another human being or animal. Even at the cinema I cannot stand the sight of a surgical operation or even injection, and accidents, blood, or wounds are worse. . . . It was a catastrophe for me when I found I was pregnant. . . .

However, things being as they were, I had to choose a clinic, I had read articles on childbirth without pain and had heard a broadcast on one of these confinements. The method seemed intelligent and logical. It appealed to me greatly. One thing made me hesitate. I had no confidence in myself. Though the method was excellent for women of normal sensibilities, could it be used for me?

Yet by traditional methods, I was sure to suffer. The new method left me with a hope, a chance. If it failed, it could not be worse than other systems. . . . I worked hard, did what I was told and followed the doctor's lectures with greatest interest.

I was advised not to see the film [on natural childbirth], but something made me go. I took the risk; either this would finish me or would do me a lot of good.

It did me a lot of good. I, who cannot stand seeing an injection, easily stood the sight of this childbirth because it was obvious that the woman did not suffer.

From 4:30 A.M. to 8:30 P.M. on November 9 she handled her own contractions with a trip to and from the nursing home around 10 A.M. during a period when contractions had stopped.

5:30 P.M.: I failed once or twice to synchronize the contraction and the breathing, and I noticed that then I had pain. Between the contractions I relaxed and I breathed deeply.

I reached the nursing home at 8:25 P.M. I was examined and innocently asked the midwife if labor had started. To my great surprise, she said that I was between one-half and three-quarters dilated, and it was time to call the doctor and assistant. . . .

I began to push according to instructions. I had to make great efforts, because a few small difficulties arose. The back of the baby was to the right, the head very big, and the ligament on the right of the pelvis very hard. Also I felt no urge to push.

Anyhow, I did my best, according to what I had been taught, though at the beginning I made a few mistakes in breathing. The doctor had to help me with forceps. But there again I felt no pain. The only unpleasant thing was to have to push, to make this great muscular effort and to stand the resulting heat. At 9:15 P.M. the baby was born, one and a half hours after I had arrived at the nursing home. I had hardly felt the delivery, which I had previously imagined would be butchery. I just felt the tissues stretched painlessly. . . .

Although the forceps were used, I had no tear. I was not damaged at all. I was able to give birth without pain . . .

Psychologically, this absence of suffering had important consequences. I, who thought of the arrival of a baby as a calamity, who had no maternal instinct—because, I realize now, I was afraid of suffering—and who even thought that I could not become fond of the baby, am very happy to have him. Besides, I feel freed from an obsession. I no longer fear another childbirth.

As with hypnosis or acupuncture, researchers do not agree on how or why such prepared birth succeeds. "Verbal analgesia" (commands by doctor or midwife) combine with the woman's concentration on kinds and rhythms of breathing to distract her attention. All abdominal and uterine sensations are present; she blocks her own brain from interpreting them as pain. Use of chemical drugs, whether labor speeding or sleep inducing, can inhibit her concentration, her ability to control and ride the waves of sensation.

By now, so many couples, women, and physicians worldwide have used the Lamaze method that research has analyzed its effectiveness to reduce pain (old approach) and to promote childbirth as an exciting, even ecstatic experience (new approach). Older women, if defined as high risk, can especially profit from its use to build confidence, allay anxiety.

Motherhood and Personality is Dr. Leon Chertok's study of 96 women prepared by the psychoprophylactic method and 26 unprepared women. The book appeared in France in 1966. His goal was to evaluate the method for reducing negativity and promoting easy delivery. His conclusions for his group of prepared women:

1. The method is more effective for behavior control than for pain control. It does this by furnishing "a model of behavior to which the women try to adhere."

2. The method is most effective for women with the least negativity. At some points, the woman's individual psychology is the deciding factor: "At the most anxious moments during confinement, the women's reactions are essentially determined by their individual psychological structure, and preparation has little effect."

3. Preparation is least effective when "deep-dying inhibitions have to be dealt with."

4. Women prepared by the psychoprophylactic method have better confinements. "In particular, their behavioral control is better than that of unprepared women . . . relations with the staff of the labor ward and the first relationship to the baby were significantly better in prepared women."

By Erna Wright's own estimates in *The New Childbirth,* only 35 percent of her patients have a painless labor, although an additional 65 percent can keep pain "within tolerable limits." "Painless" does not and should not mean "sensationless," that is, anesthetized or unconscious.

But do such percentages really comfort? If two-thirds of women expect to suffer or do suffer, no wonder so many, especially older ones with longer unfortunate conditioning, may beg for anesthesia. Something remains wrong either with preparation or with the psychology that couples or women bring to it. Even the Lamaze method is now attacked as too hospital or doctor dependent, too oriented toward military-style commands and self-control.

To explain why some kinds of birth training fail, here is Marjorie Karmel's description of her (non)education prior to Lamaze training:

Before my first pregnancy I had never given any thought at all to the question of how to have a baby; I can't remember ever having heard it discussed at all, beyond the most minimal attention given it in a college hygiene course where it was almost totally eclipsed by the much more interesting question of how to conceive a baby. Therefore, the discovery of the vast quantity of intensely felt convictions and prejudices that exist on the subject came to me as something of a revelation.

And here is her description of an American discussion group-with-a-few-exercises that she attended before her second birth. She contrasts this with the effective, disciplined but friendly Lamaze training that had prepared her for the first birth:

It was all good—as far as it went. If I had had my first child knowing only that much, I would certainly have been relieved of the anxiety of having something completely unknown happen to me. On the other hand, I would have been left completely passive and dependent. There was no real step-by-step training in how to conduct your own labor. There was nothing like the feeling of confidence I got from Mme. Cohen's insistence that I would be the one who would have my baby.

Of the American birth class she told her American doctor, "It's excellent general education that ought to be given in every high school. But I don't think it really prepares you to take an active part in the birth of your child."

The doctor answers:

Girls come to me who have no idea what's going to happen to them. Some of them are scared to death. That course gives them a real sense of knowledge, a real peace of mind. They aren't all like you; many of them don't have the self-confidence to take kindly to the suggestion that having their babies is their responsibility. It wouldn't be fair to foist a single point of view on them. The object is to help everyone.

Marjorie Karmel sadly concludes:

Now I see what's wrong with the course at the hospital; it's geared to the lowest common sensibility, the most neurotic and fearful expectant mother. Granted that there should be a general education course for women who don't want anything more. Why not give the ones who do something satisfying?

The body effort of giving birth has been likened to a 9-mile swim. As an older woman, you will encounter additional prejudice that your muscles are not flexible enough, can't take the strain, etc. If you choose the Lamaze method, *you owe yourself a good teacher* who instills confidence and makes you work.

Adrienne Rich is a poet and reporter on contemporary women's lifestyles; she wrote *Of Woman Born*. She summarizes her conclusions on two styles of birth—prepared and unconscious. Her three children were born in the late Fifties, each birth conducted with general anesthesia, although only the first required it.

I think now that my refusal of consciousness (approved and implemented by my physician) and my friends' exhilaration at having experienced and surmounted pain (approved and implemented by their physicians) had a common source: we were trying in our several ways to contain and control the expected female feat of passive suffering. . . . None of us, I think, had much sense of being in any real command of the experience.

She believes "the premium should be on an active psychological experience, not on the pain endured." Birth should not be "a contest to see how much you can take."

Current attitudes stress the value of Lamaze techniques in making birth a pleasurable, even cosmic, experience —and only one aspect of a woman's or couple's whole psychosexual development.

Results of psychologist Dr. Deborah Tanzer's work appeared as *Why Natural Childbirth?* in 1972. Her conclusion: The most pleasurable births occur *only* when the woman shares the experience with another adult close to her—husband, friend.

My study also revealed the great benefits of the husbands' participation. Their presence at delivery was essential to their wives' feelings of rapture and contributed in a major way to their wives' more positive perceptions of themselves and the world. The husbands of the natural childbirth group were responded to more positively and perceived as strong and helpful in contrast to the husbands of the control group who were often seen by their wives as weak and helpless.

Dr. Tanzer stresses birth as a function of personal power or responsibility and, thereby, a political act. "People have so little control over so many important aspects of their lives that it is little wonder that birth, too, is accepted as just another alienated experience. . . . Women now approach birth with far less education and training than is required for any other major event in their lives."

DR. LEBOYER WITHOUT VIOLENCE

Children's rights advocates insist that sensitivity to birth as parental experience is valuable but misses the goal of the occasion—giving the baby an entrance that is also safe, peaceful, loving.

This is the basic idea of Dr. Frederick Leboyer, who has delivered over 1,000 babies using birth without violence (and over 7,000 before he evolved the method).

He is a dynamic, informal, gray-haired man who speaks enthusiastically. His rules are simple and humane. Assuming a normal delivery, the moment the child emerges, (s)he is placed on the mother's abdomen, stroked and calmed—instead of dangled by the legs and forced to scream. After the cord is cut, the quiet child is stroked further in a warm bath. The delivery room remains silent and dimly lit. A calm child is a happy child who has already begun to trust the world and adults. The whole procedure takes only minutes.

However, unlike babies, adults are not at all calm about Dr. Leboyer! Several European and American obstetricians have cited fear of infection, if not death, from dunking the newly cut umbilicus into water and postponing careful examination. Attacking Leboyer as some *nouveau* Rousseau, they ridicule or fear the poetic, mystical language in his book *Birth Without Violence*. In any case, they are underwhelmed by his Freudian insistence on birth trauma.

Dr. Leboyer does not believe in older couples or women aged 40 to 45 having babies. He does not even want the father in the delivery room—a stand that aroused strong disagreement at the conference I attended. The father, like the obstetrician, is there, he believes, only because the mother herself is still a child, lacks confidence or skill to perform comforting tasks herself. "I feel only the mother and child should be there because basically the woman is having a love experience not with her husband but with cosmic, orgasmic forces."

Dr. Leboyer expressed no interest in helping progressive Americans institute reforms. Q: "Tell us how to start a movement. Will you communicate with us?" A: "Don't communicate with me. Communicate with babies! The right people will meet. Things happen."

I left the conference depressed, concluding that Dr. Leboyer sabotages his own ideas by acting so unconcerned about their "packaging"—outspoken sometimes, frustratingly reticent otherwise. Example: "What is your opinion on episiotomy?" "I feel that giving my opinion in this country would be disrespectful."

If a baby is born with his umbilicus wrapped around his neck, it is obvious that we don't sing a mystical song. We cut it. If a baby's life is in danger because he has difficulty breathing, we reanimate him immediately, of course. And we turn the lights on. And if a baby is seen to spit up heavy mucus substances, naturally we suck them out with a probe. What we do not do is to employ all the instruments as a *matter of routine* as other doctors do "just in case." All this technical monkey business during birth represents only our own fears of being inadequate should trouble arise.

Emphasizing the child, Dr. Leboyer appears to neglect the mother, but in practice his method depends on a calm, cooperating woman. Marie-France Han, 34, a sales manager for a French film company, delivered her first child with Dr. Leboyer:

I lay in the delivery room quite conscious and aware. The room was dim, but it was dawn and you could see the sun coming through the window. The atmosphere Dr. Leboyer created was quiet and meditative, like a church. Things were serious but joyous. I felt as though a ritual were going to take place. The doctor was marvelously helpful during labor, but at the moment of birth he became just as interested in my baby as in me. When I cried out in happiness and excitement, he quickly calmed me because it is not good for the newborn to hear loud noises. I must be serene and quiet to welcome my baby, he told me.

Then he put my daughter on my stomach for as long as the umbilical cord continued to function. He massaged the baby and he let me help with my own hands. During the whole time Dr. Leboyer was singing a soft, repetitive Indian melody of some kind. Gradually I could feel my baby relax under his soothing massage and become calmer. She cried only a little bit. Then he gave her a long bath in warm water. The delivery was one of the most important, happiest moments of my life.

Mothers of several children report that Leboyer babies are "gay, open, easily satisfied." And psychologists confirm that these children are "spared nearly all the major and minor psychopathologies—of eating, sleeping, maternal relations, etc.—of infancy." These are opinions furnished by Dr. Leboyer during his U.S. tour.

Older parents with only one or one more chance at parenthood want to know, How can we do it right or better than we did before? While controversial and not for everyone, Dr. Leboyer's simple techniques provide one answer. They will survive (after initial skirmishes) for a simple reason—they work. They calm the conscious infant just as Lamaze and related methods have educated and strengthened women to remain awake and aware. At the most, they will alert doctors and parents who do not yet realize that newborns have emotional, as well as physical, needs. Birth is stressful; infant crying is a natural response to stress. The point is never to let it become an unheeded yell of terror.

Other physicians are already testing how to lower the "shock" of birth for all babies but especially for the premature. Dr. Louis Gluck, a pediatrician at University Hospital, San Diego, is combining use of waterbed mattresses in incubators with recordings of maternal heartbeats. Both these features merely simulate the uterine environment the baby has just left. Dr. Gluck says, "The babies seem to feed better, sleep better, and have fewer periods when they forget to breathe—which is the biggest occupational hazard in caring for premature babies."

THE PSYCHOSEXUAL METHOD

Sheila Kitzinger is a British anthropologist and mother of five children. She has combined Read and Lamaze techniques plus Stanislavsky's body training for actors into her own method. Her books, especially *The Experience of Childbirth*, are already into several editions. The National Childbirth Trust in London now trains Kitzinger teachers, and Mrs. Kitzinger lectures occasionally in the U.S. and Canada.

Her work includes psychological preparation, couple counseling, "touch relaxation," and vivid (sexual, womanly) descriptions of what birth feels like. The touch method is guided growth in relaxation through a set of special exercises. The woman conditions herself (or is conditioned by whoever monitors labor, usually her husband) first to tense sets of muscles, then to release and relax. "The husband who is alert and sensitive to see the buildup of tension, however slight, can rest his hand on the muscles involved, both between contractions, and, if she wishes it, at the onset of contractions."

Before women have had a child, they often think that childbirth entails a great deal of pushing and straining and that therefore the really important purpose of prenatal exercise is that one should develop very strong abdominal muscles. . . . But after they have had a baby they realize that it is more a matter of breathing and coordination.

Many women find that the harmony they create between the contractions and their breathing gives them real delight. Even when the contractions are very fierce—at the end of the first stage of labor when the cervix of the uterus is almost fully dilated . . . it is possible for labour to be pleasurable, much like swimming in a stormy sea. . . .

The mother feels the pressure of the baby's head against the rectum as it proceeds still lower and reaches the deepest point in the arch of its journey. It feels very much like a grapefuit. . . . The woman begins to feel herself gradually opening up, like a bud into full flower, a strange experience which may be rather frightening for an unprepared woman. This may be accompanied by a warm tingling sensation. Some women hate it; they find it what can only be described as "shocking." For the conscious woman who is participating actively in labor, the moment when the head crowns is an intensely pleasurable and very exciting one.

How do pregnant couples and teachers respond to the Kitzinger method?

Ann Gray of International Childbirth Education Association, Inc. (ICEA), McLean, Virginia, wrote me:

I feel all the childbirth educators (approximately 100) who attended the workshop Sheila Kitzinger

did here last year [1974] have incorporated aspects
of her method into their own teaching. In particular,
touch relaxation was readily adopted. As Mrs.
Kitzinger says, it is a highly individualized approach;
some teachers will be comfortable and effective using certain techniques, while others won't.

It is always hard to define "success" and "failure"
with regard to childbirth, but I think most childbirth
educators feel Mrs. Kitzinger's approach to sexuality
and her emphasis on body awareness and relaxation
are very effective. Personally I found her touch relaxation technique extremely beneficial for the birth
of my third child seven months ago.

HUSBAND-COACHED BIRTH

Dr. Robert Bradley is an obstetrician who believes that
husbands are the logical and ideal companions to most
women during birth. He feels that doctors receive the
gratitude, hugs, or kisses from women who have happily
delivered only because husbands are not asserting their
prior rights to these joyful expressions.

Dr. Bradley has a national address in California (see
Appendix IV), and classes in his method are held in some
large cities. Teacher training is also available.

Wherever husbands, trained or untrained, are still considered infectious intruders into labor and delivery is
good territory for publicizing the Bradley method. Even
the educated or trained husband may encounter resist-
ance—unless the couple has chosen a cooperative doctor.

Here are sentences from the HILADS form (Husbands
in Labor and Delivery Suite) that I got during a prenatal
course at my local hospital. Chiefly it makes certain that
the husband knows when to enter, when to leave. And he
is ordered to leave just when the woman most needs him
—if there's a problem.

Recently increasing numbers of husbands have
been trained to provide support during labor and delivery. As a result, it has been possible for many
men to coach their wives in labor, and in some
cases, to be present at delivery as well. Naturally, if

his wife is heavily medicated or is asleep for delivery, the husband will leave. . . .

It is important to remember that many women do not wish to be awake during labor, and these women receive medication and anesthesia which is designed to block their awareness of sensation of labor, and they react entirely differently to labor. They may be noisy at times, but this does not indicate that anything is wrong. . . .

It is impossible to predict the emotional reaction of a man watching his wife give birth to a child. The husband must understand that there is no one to take care of him if the experience is more than he can cope with. Thus, he accompanies his wife to the delivery room at his own risk.

One of the "Orders of the Day" below which he signs:

While in the delivery room, I will remain seated on the stool at the head of the table. If my wife receives heavy medication in labor or anesthesia for delivery, I will leave the labor and delivery area.

When I asked the labor room nurse giving our group tour the reason for this last injunction, she said, "It's because the anesthetist needs the husband's stool to sit on." Ah, so. . . .

Jane, a friend in her early thirties, described that moment when her husband was asked to leave. Both had attended Lamaze classes. She was delivering her first baby with a woman doctor thoughtfully chosen at a famous Manhattan hospital. First-stage labor (dilatation), aided by pitocin (oxytocin) tablets dissolved in her mouth, proceeded adequately. Second-stage labor (expulsion) did not. After two hours of second stage, the doctor applied forceps; the baby appeared. Then Jane, conscious throughout, hemorrhaged. Transfusions began. Someone asked her husband to leave.

She remembers, "That was the absolute worst moment. I felt abandoned. If only somebody had told me ahead of time he could be asked to leave. All that went through my head was, Well, he's got the baby now, my job's over, I don't matter anymore."

Jane's comment on her Lamaze class: "I talked with

the other women afterward; none of us felt we did very well. In my case, contractions increased with such intensity there was no chance to relax or breathe or anything else between them. When it came to expelling the baby, I just felt swamped and exhausted."

The frustration of such stories is that no one can prove that had labor not been drug accelerated (which increases the intensity of the contractions), she might have coped better with the late first stage and not collapsed just before expulsion. The hemorrhage could have been caused by either forceps or uterine atony (muscular weakness) in the presence of obstructed labor. Doctors generally agree on a 2-hour period as the maximum in which to achieve expulsion of a first baby, one hour for a second. Beyond these times, the risks are infant death and rupture of the thinning uterine walls.

The usual postnatal explanation is that first births are such a concatenation and multiplication of unknowns that anything can happen. From the doctor's viewpoint the fault lies, if anywhere, with the woman's body. However, Jane and her husband survived and are now parents of a healthy 2-year-old son.

By contrast, here is a humane and trusting evaluation of father participation by Dr. Michael Goodman of Ft. Bragg, California. He is a veteran of over 1,000 deliveries —600 with father present.

The fathers were an amazingly diverse group, from long-haired members of the counterculture to corporate VPs to loggers, including both men well trained in childbirth preparation and men who decided to go in at the last minute.

However, almost without exception, they had one thing in common: They were a great help to their women, were elated and elevated by the experience, and in the process, I think felt much closer to their newborn child. . . . In fact, when I am expecting a bad time or difficult delivery, this is the time when I especially encourage the father's participation, for it is at this time that the mother needs all the extra support she can get.

Any physician who is secure in his position and medically competent should not fear the father's presence at *any* time in the delivery room. (From *Obstetrics-Gynecology News,* May 15, 1975.)

In 1974 the House of Representatives received a bill to make it illegal for a hospital to bar a father's participation if his wife desires it. When it passes, no longer will a father have to handcuff himself to the delivery table (Chicago) or be charged with disorderly conduct and fined (Union, N.J.) if he wishes to be present at his child's birth.

CHAPTER 16

More Methods:
Oldest to Newest

IN APRIL, 1975, U.S. TV VIEWERS SAW A Chinese woman awake and waving toward the camera while her doctor performed a Caesarean and lifted out the live baby. The startling feature: Her only anesthesia was acupuncture. The film was Shirley MacLaine's *The Other Side of the Sky: A China Memoir.* How many acupuncture needles the mother received or where in her body the doctor had inserted them was not announced.

The basic acupuncture technique consists of precise insertion of numerous needles along networks ("meridians") of points on the skin. For each point or series of points, a corresponding body part is affected. The needles, twirled or rotated, remain some minutes. You feel the skin pricked, but there is no bleeding. The needles do not touch or injure nerves. The pain site and the site for insertion of needles may be the same or different. For neck or spinal pain, a patient receives needles along the spine and between finger joints. As with Lamaze breathing techniques, the needle process temporarily inhibits the nerves' ability to transmit pain sensations from pain site to brain.

And what are the neurologic mechanics of this?

The most common explanation is the "gate theory." Pain reaches the brain through two major centers, one in the brain, the other in the spinal cord. Manipulating the needles floods or overloads these "gates" with such a burst of impulses that they temporarily cease further transmission. Acupuncture also increases blood circulation to the pain site.

The Chinese doctor or acupuncturist studies and practices for six years before final certification. For centuries the Chinese have combined acupuncture with herbal medicine to relieve pain and discomfort. Since 1966 they have begun to blend it with Western-style surgery. They have now performed nearly a half million operations, including major heart-lung surgery, with acupuncture as the only anesthesia.

In 1971 a Chinese doctor in Peking treated James Reston, *New York Times* editorial writer, by acupuncture for severe gastritis (stomach pain) following emergency appendectomy. The appendectomy itself had been done with Western (chemical) anesthesia. The acupuncturist inserted three long needles into Reston's elbow and lower legs. After about 20 minutes the stomach pain stopped. Of acupuncture, Reston reported, "It's not at all painful. It tingles a bit, but that's about all."

In ancient China, male doctors did not examine nude female patients; midwives aided births. However, acupuncturists did insert needles into correct points to treat stomach or back complaints of pregnancy.

How does acupuncture aid in childbirth? When done by a skilled physician, it is a safe procedure. It should interest anyone who seeks alternate means of delivery free from the side effects of drugs on mother and baby.

In 1973 a Washington, D.C., woman, already the mother of two Caesarean children, had a third using acupuncture, instead of general or spinal anesthesia, for the Caesarean surgery. In March 1973 a Chicago news reporter, Linda Lee Landis, had a normal vaginal birth with acupuncture. When I questioned a representative at the Acupuncture Information Center of New York in Manhattan, she told me that doctors in California are currently using acupuncture for some labor and delivery. In California it is a cooperative endeavor. The acupuncturist inserts needles at the time when local anesthesia is desired. The obstetrician remains responsible for the woman's total care. On the East Coast, use of acupuncture awaits "interesting and educating obstetricians."

HYPNOTHERAPY

Hypnosis is another of humanity's oldest forms of mind and body control. If you seek delivery without anesthesia but for some reason doubt your ability to withstand pain, hypnosis is a good technique to investigate. You may use it with or without Lamaze training, although Lamaze classes also teach relaxation.

Hypnosis training of patients takes longer, which is why many obstetricians have discarded it. However, it is the one form of prenatal conditioning—other than Sheila Kitzinger's broad psychosexual approach—which is transferable to other life situations. Increasing will power, acquiring positive habits of thought are valuable no matter what your later work. And a calm parent is a useful addition to any household.

Like the Lamaze method, hypnosis involves a state of aroused, intense concentration. And your willingness to learn is just as crucial to its success. Hypnosis also creates increased susceptibility to suggestion from a person you trust. Some hypnotherapists believe it superior to the Lamaze method because it recognizes and deals with a woman's unconscious or otherwise hidden ambivalence or worries about pregnancy and birth—whatever constricts muscles and creates tension for her. Like other methods, success requires cooperation by you as a couple, your doctor, and the hypnotist.

Most hypnosis is private, individual "tutoring." However, some obstetricians, like Dr. William S. Kroger of Beverly Hills, California, have combined group preparation (2 hours twice a month) with a series of six individual sessions to teach women the basic hypnotic techniques.

What happens if you consult such a therapist?

(S)he assesses your ability to be hypnotized, initially by the therapist, then by yourself. *You learn to hypnotize yourself.* The physician or therapist first asks you to concentrate, perhaps stare at a spot on the ceiling or wall. Your eyelids become heavy at the suggestion to relax (light hypnosis). If you consent to go deeper, the therapist will ask you to do something, perhaps raise an arm over your head and stiffen it. In this second stage (medium hypnosis) your eyes remain shut and you can keep the suggested arm posture for as long as asked. You do not feel your arm "heavy" or "stiff"; indeed, it seems to grow lighter as you relax further.

By will, suggestion, and relaxation you can thus numb any part of your body. It is a technique you can practice at home between sessions when you sit quietly and teach yourself to numb your hand, for example, and transfer this insensitivity to pain onto your abdomen or back, wherever you desire. This is called "glove anesthesia."

In deep hypnosis (third stage) your eyes are open; you are completely relaxed. At various points during the process the therapist speaks positive suggestions, perhaps, "My body is functioning normally. . . . I am at peace about what is happening to my body. . . . When the doctor touches me on my forehead (or wherever) I will relax deeper."

For more than 25 years Lynne Gordon, hypnotherapist and executive director of the Hypnosis Center, Manhattan, has worked with people desiring hypnosis to treat personal problems. She has been a consultant in medical hypnosis in New York hospitals and clinics for cases involving speech and eye disorders and various other emotional and psychological difficulties. For each patient she chooses a "key word," available for posthypnotic suggestion once the person has returned to usual awareness. For a mother of three expecting another baby and experiencing constant impatience with the children's demands, Lynne Gordon used "I love you"—practiced and conditioned until with each burst of impatience toward a child came also a burst of "I love you" with its attendant peace and relaxation. In some cases she gives the woman's doctor a "posthypnotic key" (word or touch) in addition to what the woman has received.

In Chapter 10 I described the use of hypnosis to combat fears of pregnancy and birth and quoted letters from one of Lynne Gordon's patients and her obstetrician. She has also conditioned couples with psychological infertility as well as groups of pregnant women. She told me, "I teach autosuggestion and self-hypnosis to my clients. I work with people troubled by obesity, smoking, sexual difficulties. You know, pregnant women can have all these, too, besides being pregnant. I help them ease tension, relax, and be confident. I help them discover the adventure and pleasure of the prenatal period and having a baby—the fun and joy of it."

Lynne Gordon, who has given lectures and demonstrations around the world, is a member of the professional division of the American Institute of Hypnosis. News articles have called her "the first female hypnotist publicly known throughout the world."

Mrs. M.E., one of Dr. Kroger's patients, gives this account of her experiences:

In August I gave birth to a 6 pound, 13 1/2 ounce baby boy while under hypnosis, and it was a memorable experience. Having had practically no illness during my childhood, I had developed a fear of doctors and hospitals. Yet, due to the conditioning period during my maternity visits to the doctor's office, I entered the hospital with absolutely no nervous feeling of any kind in connection with the delivery.

The personal attention of my doctor, such as his use of my first name, helped create the feeling of self-confidence. . . . Knowing that the doctor and my husband would be present during the labor period also gave me an added feeling of relaxation.

The hypnosis in my case was administered via the telephone during the first stages of labor. Though I was not in a private labor room and had to witness other women's reactions, I still did not feel any apprehension. I had a sense of detachment. Though the pain was present, my body was relaxed. I was fully aware of the surroundings, and was able to inquire, while in the delivery room, as to the sex of my baby, and whether he was in good health. A complete feeling of exhilaration followed. . . .

Four years later I gave birth to my second son. . . . This delivery with hypnosis was even more effective because of the confidence I had developed from my first child's birth.

As with Lamaze, labor and delivery sensations were fully present. However, she did not experience them as a crisis of pain and anxiety.

Hypnosis involves work, self-discipline, meditation—and none of those is "magic"! Mrs. R. B. wrote Dr. Kroger: "I find myself amused at the doubts and frustrations I experienced during attendance at your classes, and in my experiments with self-hypnosis at home. You see, I tried to make more of a mystery of hypnosis than it really is. I must even confess that I was disappointed when I first discovered that there was no 'magic' involved."

In 1958 the AMA approved hypnosis for medical use. To locate a qualified hypnotherapist, especially one with medical training, you may write to the American Society of Clinical Hypnosis, 2400 East Devon, Suite 218, Des Plaines, Illinois 60018. Lynne Gordon's Hypnosis Center is 160 West 73 St., New York 10023.

NEWEST DEVICES

One reason a first labor is lengthy is that the cervix (neck of the womb) dilates slowly, compared with later births. The laboring cervix is pulled open by contraction of muscles running the length of the uterus. When the cervix has stretched to about 10 cm. in diameter—4 inches or 5 male fingers wide—the dilatation stage of labor is over; expulsion can begin.

The process resembles easing an object, such as a ball, out of the elasticized mouth of a stocking by tightening your hand. This squeezes both ball and stocking from behind. A Swiss study found that a first labor averages 135 of these contractions or "squeezes," later labors average 68.

Doctors in Japan, England, and Sweden have developed vibratorlike devices that relax the cervix by mechanical means. They are valuable for patients with heart or lung problems—any woman whose body cannot endure a long labor—and for cases of slow or intermittent labor with fetal distress.

In Japan a cervical vibrator has increased dilatation from 2 to 6 cm. in an average of one minute by relaxing rigid muscle and tissue. Average duration for a first labor is only 5 to 6 hours, with 2 to 4 hours for later labors.

In LaCrosse, Wisconsin, a neurosurgeon, Dr. C. Norman Shealy, has developed a device called the "transcutaneous nerve stimulator." Its most famous user? Governor George Wallace, to alleviate pain from his spinal injuries.

An obstetrician, Dr. William J. O'Leary, has now applied it to female labor. Of 39 women, 31 reported "extremely favorable results" and would use it again. With it, no woman needed anesthesia or analgesia during labor, and about one-quarter of the women needed only local anesthesia (pudendal block) during successful deliveries. The device is most effective for early labor involving back (rather than abdominal) discomfort. A woman using it feels and hears a vibrating, buzzing sound from the two stimulator electrodes fastened to her back.

BABIES BY DECOMPRESSION

At first, the decompression method—and its vacuum cleaner-like "birth bubble"—seem surrealistic. However, if as an older woman, you have high blood pressure or other vascular problem, decompression is worth investigating.

The equipment was devised in Johannesburg, South Africa, by Dr. O. S. Heyns for use by "high risk" women with maternal or fetal circulatory problems. It is now used in several Western countries, including the U.S. and Great Britain, by itself or combined with Lamaze training. It assists any case in which the fetus's supply of oxygen, which is dependent on maternal blood flow and functioning placenta, is insufficient not only during labor but during pregnancy as well.

About 1970, controversy about the decompression method filled the letters columns of medical journals, probably because too much was claimed initially either by its originators or by journalists. Employing it will not produce a high I.Q. baby, but it can do much to ensure a shortened, undrugged labor and healthy newborn.

Basic equipment is an airtight fiberglass suit with bucket seat that fits around the middle of a woman's body. Her arms and legs are free. Air suction through a hose reduces atmospheric pressure (one-half ton at sea level, 14.7 pounds per square inch) on her abdomen. The air is simply vacuumed out from inside the suit. Reduced air pressure expands the abdominal wall, lifting it off the uterus. The woman controls the process by consulting a pressure gauge in front of her and opening or closing a vent with her thumb.

The South African doctors tested the equipment on themselves first—and experienced no ill effects on their abdomens from prolonged periods at various low pressures, such as one-half or two-thirds full atmosphere.

A woman uses Dr. Heyns' equipment for one or two brief sessions before her twentieth week of pregnancy. She has three sessions between the twenty-fourth and twenty-seventh weeks. From the twenty-eighth week to delivery, she uses it twice daily at home or clinic. Its documented advantages during pregnancy: relaxation, easing muscle strain and backache, alleviating varicose veins, preventing toxemia, and preventing miscarriage due to placental insufficiency.

One woman said, "I can be taut and irritable, really just a bundle of nerves, so tired but at the same time so high-strung that I can't begin to sleep, and after even a half hour of decompression, I can feel all the tightness and tension melting away."

One of obstetrician Heyns' most unusual patients was a male rugby player whose back was injured during a game. The player was decompressed in the maternity ward of Queen Victoria Maternity Hospital, and his pain soon abated. The probable reason: One cause of back pain (other than broken bones or injured nerves, which he did not have) is muscle spasm. Decompression expands the rib cage, moving the muscles, breaking the spasm.

A woman obviously cannot remain in the decompression suit for delivery, but how does it work during labor? A woman timing her own progress increases decompression when she feels a contraction beginning and decreases it when over.

Dr. Heyns reports an average labor of only 4 hours for first babies, and 77 percent of his patients in one group experienced "excellent relief from pain with decompression and without anesthesia. Instead of having an exhausted, squeezed out rag of a patient, you have a woman who is physically and emotionally alert and excited about the whole adventure. She is truly energized."

In Canada Dr. Louis J. Quinn of St. Mary's Hospital,

Montreal, reported that of 46 patients, only 8 had less than what they termed "good relief" of pain.

Among many high-risk patients (with histories of stroke or miscarriage, for example) treated by Dr. L. E. Lundgren, Houston, Texas, was Mrs. T, 38 years old, with a weight of 220 pounds, blood pressure of 180/120. During her first trimester of pregnancy, despite bed rest, diuretic and other medication to decrease blood pressure, Mrs. T's condition deteriorated. When her pressure reached 220/120, her tissues swelled with edema.

At 5 months Dr. Lundgren started her on one hour daily of decompression. When her blood pressure dropped, he increased decompression to 2 hours daily. Soon Mrs. T's pressure was down to 190/110, although medication except for diuretics had been halved, then discontinued. However, it is normal for the blood pressures of pregnant women, even hypertensive patients, to drop during the second trimester.

Dr. Lundgren reported, "When she was checked at weekly intervals the blood pressure kept decreasing, so that by the seventh month the patient's pressure averaged about 140/90. . . After a 5-hour labor, during which her blood pressure was 130/90, she delivered a male with an Apgar score of 10 [pink baby, excellent condition]. It's interesting to note that after the baby was delivered and Mrs. T had discontinued decompression, her blood pressure went right back up."

Sheila Kitzinger wrote me her opinion on the use of this equipment in Britain:

I think the main value of the decompression suit is when there are small-for-date babies since it allows the placenta to function much more effectively. It was invented in South Africa, as you know, and is still being used in the Queen Victoria Hospital, Johannesburg. The idea that it produces more intelligent children has now been discredited.

It certainly does make contractions less painful. But the big snag there is that the woman has to be unzipped from it in order to be examined, and many patients find this disturbing. Some women also find it extremely hot to be inside a plastic bag throughout labor. I have only had a few women who have been to my classes and also used the decompression suit, and they have all said that breathing helped as much as or more than the suit, and all eventually discarded it as they reached 7 or 8 cms. because they felt they could cope with contractions without so much disturbance then.

The South African doctors have now developed modified equipment for use during delivery to meet the unzipping problem. It is a hand-held dome that fits over the pelvic area, including vagina. It was invented primarily to ease distressed infants out quickly without need of forceps.

BIRTH HOMES AND THE POLITICS OF MIDWIFERY

Some older women I interviewed, especially those expecting a second or later baby and a probably quick, normal birth, were annoyed at doctors who will consider delivery only in a hospital. If you feel this way, there is now an alternative.

This is the birth home (different from birth *at* home) where you are attended by a midwife with a doctor available. The two I learned about—the first of their kind in the U.S.—are Booth Memorial Home, Philadelphia, and the Maternity Center Association Home, Manhattan. Mrs. Ruth Lubic, head of the Association, directs the New York home. The Manhattan program, in 1975, cost about $550 for prenatal services, education for birth and infant care, labor and delivery, all examinations. This state-licensed home takes only women expected to have normal, uncomplicated deliveries, and admission is presently limited to New York City residents. The advantages are a homey setting in which a woman can labor and deliver surrounded by her family. She can take any medically safe position for delivery and can forego the routine enema, shaving, or episiotomy. She may leave with her baby 12 hours after birth if she chooses. A pediatrician examines the baby before discharge, and visiting nurses check maternal and infant progress on the first, third, and fifth days home.

Nurse-midwives are skilled and licensed to handle normal births. Many couples find a midwife more positive and encouraging than an obstetrician whose training has emphasized the abnormal, the crisis, the cliffhanger situation. Helen, a midwife from California, said to me, "There is no need for an obstetrician at normal births, However, his skill at rapid assessment of difficult cases, his knowledge of drugs and surgical procedures is invaluable at the right time, at crisis points. But the majority of births are not this four-alarm medical crisis, and rarely has he spent long enough with the woman to provide the comfort and reassurance she needs to help her deliver *her* child."

Another possibility is delivery in a hospital with a midwife. For several years, at least four New York hospitals —Kings County in Brooklyn, Roosevelt Hospital, Jacobi Hospital, Beth Israel Medical Center—have used teams of midwives to provide prenatal care and deliver thousands of babies.

The immense service the midwife renders is that she remains with you *throughout* labor and delivery. She does not pop in during the last hour or 5 minutes mainly to catch the baby and sew you up.

Pediatrician Lee Salk writes, "These days it seems that midwives perform more and more deliveries. When I ask parents who have selected a midwife rather than an obstetrician why they made that choice, they often report that the midwives seemed to have more compassion and human understanding than the doctors they had met."

Unfortunately, in some states, nurse-midwives are still not allowed to practice in or outside hospitals. Nurse-midwives trained at Johns Hopkins, Baltimore, still cannot practice in Maryland, for example, driving people who desire this style of birth even farther beyond the system.

OUTSIDE THE ESTABLISHMENT

It is a contemporary fact that many couples, young or older, leery of anesthesia, surgery, or bureaucracy, are rejecting the hospital birth that has become the norm for the Western world. They are choosing to deliver at home by themselves or with a midwife or brave doctors not deterred by the furor over malpractice insurance. I do not recommend this for the older couple involved in their *first* pregnancy or for any older woman with severe medical problems.

The problem with home delivery is not that it's "new"

(old). The difficulties happen because the U.S., unlike Britain with its "flying squad" ambulance services, lacks back-up facilities to treat a laboring or delivering woman, should her care become complicated. The one exception to this I learned about was in Cook County, Illinois, outside Chicago, where properly equipped squad services do support home births.

However, the views of some people with wide experience of normal birth are valuable on the topics of nutrition and home management of pregnancy, if not of birth. People like Norman Casserley, the only lay male midwife in the U.S., are refreshing, comforting to interview because they make birth seem a natural event—a loving process for the average family to *enjoy*—instead of an anxiety- or pathology-ridden marathon for a team of contestants with a normal baby as the (sur)prise.

Conservative medical opinions can and do prevent trouble in some high-risk cases. However, not every woman over 35 is automatically high risk.

Mr. Casserley is a dapper, pleasant Irishman, 47 years old, a veteran of more than 3,500 births in all 50 states and 50 countries over the last 28 years. I interviewed him in Tarrytown, New York, after Dr. Leboyer's conference on birth without violence.

Mr. Casserley did premed at the National University of Ireland, delivered 1,000 babies in Rotunda Hospital, Dublin, and then ended his formal medical training because he refused to speed childbirth by surgery or drugs. He lives with his families for a week before and after each birth. His fees are proportional to family income.

In 1935, 65 percent of American babies were born at home with midwives or doctors. Currently only 4 percent are. In the Netherlands and Scandinavia, which regularly lead the world in low infant-mortality rates, home births are encouraged for uncomplicated cases. By contrast, with our emphasis on hospital births but relatively little provision for adequate prenatal care, the U.S. ranks sixteenth in infant mortality.

Casserley plans his schedule to see each pregnant woman and her family for three days per month. He believes pregnancy is a healthful condition involving three basic requirements: diet, exercise, and attitude. Along with nutrition suggestions, he prescribes exercise "in reasonable amounts"—walking and jogging—with sufficient rest plus techniques to strengthen the perineum, the floor of the pelvis. He teaches the couple physiology, anatomy, massage, and breathing.

Once the baby is safely born, he advocates immediate breast-feeding to help prevent hemorrhage, the chief maternal killer, by contracting the muscles of the uterus. None of Casserley's 3,500 mothers has died from hemorrhage, infection, or other birth-related crisis. His "clients" have included subteen and teen-age girls originally scheduled for Caesarean surgery and women in their midforties.

On attitude: He's a strong believer in the body's natural ability to maintain and repair itself. He advocates interference by drugs or surgery only if an abnormal condition has been scientifically diagnosed—work for a physician. For example, to prevent maternal or fetal infection and stress, he avoids vaginal and rectal digital examinations toward the end of pregnancy. "I never check for dilatation manually because I live with the family at that time, and there's no reason to know the exact day and hour of delivery." He has delivered larger than normal babies and premature babies afflicted with hyaline membrane lung disease (HMD), which can be fatal.

Traveling by Greyhound or airplane, Casserley has never missed a birth for one of his clients. During 1971 he delivered one baby per day. He has been both fined and jailed. Having a baby at home in Ohio, for example, is considered "a public nuisance." In San Diego, California, he was sentenced to 1,750 years in prison (6 months for each baby); he served one day in 1971.

At the end of our interview, my husband asked Mr. Casserley whether he is married. "I'm too young!" he announced. "And besides, I already have 3,500 children."

ORGANIZATIONS AND REFORMERS

Birth groups or advisers exist to help you discover appropriate facilities and personnel to achieve the kind of birth *you* want. As an adult, you are used to decisions in other areas of your life. There is little reason now why your medical care, especially birth, which involves the whole family, should be different.

One organization that helps people in the Washington,

D.C., area is Parent & Child, Inc. Here are a few sentences from its brochure:

> We are often asked whether we teach a specific method of childbirth training and whether we advocate totally non-medicated deliveries. . . .
>
> We offer what our teachers feel are the best techniques selected from the different "schools." We feel that labors vary and the effectiveness of a method can also vary; therefore, it is helpful for a couple to have more than one method to use. . . .
>
> Our teachers emphasize that the goal is not a totally unmedicated delivery for its own sake, but rather a satisfying, dignified, cooperative childbirth experience which a couple can remember always as a warm and satisfying event.

The group publishes an excellent bimonthly news pamphlet of latest trends in maternity care, advice to new parents, book reviews, helpful letters, book ordering service. Members also receive a calendar of events and access to the "Listening Ear Council." This involves more than 100 mothers who have volunteered to counsel new parents on "non-medical matters related to feeding, infant care, and adjustment to parenthood. Your Council member is available for you to call at any time."

Doris Haire of New Jersey has been termed "the woman who moved medical mountains." Her work of the last ten years has been a comparative study of hospital and birth practices around the world, especially in Scandinavia and the Netherlands, with the aim of introducing the best features of their systems into this country.

What are these features? All are hotly debated right now, but to summarize:
- no routine induction or forcing of labor
- no isolation of the mother in the labor room
- no conscious delivery in the reclining (lithotomy) position; delivery in a semisitting position
- no routine episiotomy
- no routine use of forceps
- no routine anesthesia or analgesia
- no restriction of newborns to 4-hour feedings.

Mrs. Haire and her husband, a hospital director, have

been co-presidents of the International Childbirth Education Association. In 1975 she became president of the American Foundation for Maternal and Child Health. She now initiates conferences on obstetric management attended by several hundred physicians, nurses, midwives, and mental health specialists concerned about brain damage from current practices.

I attended one of her slide programs showing facilities in some European hospitals and birth homes and talked with her afterward. Her whole message, simple and life sustaining, is that there are better and documented ways to manage obstetrics than we in the U.S. are managing (for whatever reasons), and we should seek them out.

Once you learn some facts about U.S. infant and maternal mortality rates and infant brain damage, you see why the reformers grow so passionate.

Infant Mortality under 1 Year (per 1,000 live births):

Sweden	9.6
Japan	11.7
.	.
.	.
U.S.	17.6 (sixteenth on list)
.	.
.	.
Argentina	59.6
India	60.6

Complications of prematurity cause 70 percent of infant deaths during the first month of life; 25 to 40 percent of "battered children" were originally premature babies in Isolette incubators. Only 6 to 8 percent of the general population is born prematurely. Prematurity deranges the bonding process between parents and baby.

U.S. Infant Brain Damage (includes cerebral palsy, nongenetic mental retardation, epilepsy, etc.)	30 per 1,000 live births. An estimated 67,000 babies damaged yearly during pregnancy and labor fail to survive their first month.

| U.S. Stillbirths | 65,000 annually |
| Maternal Mortality (from infection, hemorrhage, toxemia, anesthesia, Caesarean, etc.) | 5 per 1,000 pregnancies |

What can be done about any or all of these figures?

Beverly Aure, a registered nurse who is coordinator of nursing at the Madison, Wisconsin, perinatal center, says, "Visit hospital maternity wards across the United States and in each one you'll find a file containing three-by-five-inch cards.

"The cards are called 'routine obstetric orders,' which means that every patient is the same. Well, they aren't the same. On the card is how much medication to give any patient if she's dilated so much. The card is a contract between nurse and doctor that if nothing is really wrong, the nurse will follow the case."

Dr. Jack M. Schneider, obstetrician and co-director of the Madison center, adds, "The card also tells the nurse when the doctor wants to be called. There are a few doctors who want to be called on every case, right away. Some specify, 'No calls 11 P.M. to 7 A.M.' But the feeling of the vast majority of doctors is, 'Get me there on time, don't embarrass me, but don't get me there too early. And don't bother me too much before. If you bother me, be sure it's something urgent because I'm a busy, tired guy, and I have higher priorities than obstetrics—my office practice, or gynecologic surgery."

"So the nurses are delivering the intrapartum care—the care during labor and delivery—while the doctor sees patients in his office or gets a few more winks of sleep. And in virtually all American hospitals, nurses have not been formally trained to do this."

I do not include this last information in order to attack anybody. My quoted statistics are easily available in books, medical journals, government reports, although definitions of "brain damage" or contributing causes to maternal mortality do vary, like research populations, from one summary to another.

My hope is to motivate you as older expecting parents to *persist* until you get or create the care you and your child need.

CHAPTER 17

Insured Is Assured

DO YOU KNOW THAT:

1. Health expenses cost the average U.S. family about $2,000 per year?

2. Ninety-five percent of Americans have some insurance, but 50 percent of these lack major medical coverage adequate to finance a prolonged illness?

These are figures given by Dr. Marvin Belsky, a New York physician, during a 1975 television interview.

Here are further statistics announced in the early Seventies by the United Mine Workers:

24 million Americans have no health insurance

65 million lack in-hospital cost protection

89 million lack coverage of laboratory and x-ray fees

102 million lack coverage of physician office visits or house calls.

Regarding pregnancy and birth costs, one of my respondents in Maryland wrote me, "Our insurance covered nothing." Another in New York State wrote, "We have Blue Cross. We shall see." A third near Boston: "My IBM plan (I was on maternity leave) covered everything plus 6 weeks full pay under sickness and accident benefits." My Canadian respondent was also happy with her coverage of twins and Caesarean surgery through the Canadian government plan.

Some other insurance comments were: "As a farmer's wife, I had none," and "Everything adequate—except no prenatal coverage."

With so many U.S. health insurance reform plans, such as the Kennedy-Corman bill, the AMA plan, etc., now under discussion or legislation, it is evident some people are unhappy with the cost or coverage they now get. Without detailing the plans, it's safe to say that the two main approaches involve strengthening the existing combination of private care (fee for service) and some public services (clinic, Medicare, Medicaid) versus revolutionizing these into a health plan with increased attention to still neglected populations—rural, poor, elderly, preschoolers.

If you are expecting a child, you probably have received some physician or hospital services already and will need to decide about more. You deserve to know what and how much your insurance company will cover and what will be your responsibility.

New items or tests like amniocentesis may require special negotiation. Many doctors feel that insurance companies will not cover these supposedly "extra" expenses until parents exert more pressure. One director of a genetics unit told me, "Most insurance plans don't pay for amniocentesis yet. They don't understand it. However, some do. HIP of New York will pay most of it. Blue-Shield is variable. It's not in the contract. It seems to depend on the clerk."

Insurance reformers are investigating further areas vital to pregnant women: getting pregnancy declared a "temporary disability" (to allow operation of sick-leave benefits that male employees receive) and forbidding the mandatory leave policies that force pregnant women, regardless of emotional or physical ability, to end work at some fixed date before delivery. On January 21, 1974, the Supreme Court ruled that female public school teachers in Cleveland could not be forced to take long maternity leaves. In late 1975 the court reversed a Utah decision that had refused 18 weeks of jobless benefits to Mary Ann Turner during her last trimester and 6 weeks following delivery. The American Civil Liberties Union represented Mrs. Turner in Washington.

A 1974 survey, conducted by Prentice-Hall and the

American Society for Personnel Administration, revealed that of 1,000 companies polled, only 17.8 percent still admitted to mandatory leave policies. The guidelines for the research were those compiled by the Equal Employment Opportunity Commission in March, 1972.

Liberalized company policies should allow a woman:

1. Shorter leave before childbirth with the exact date determined by consultation between the employee and her physician regarding her fitness for work.

2. Longer leave after birth, up to 3 to 6 months without loss of seniority or other benefits.

3. Pregnancy and birth covered like other sick-leave expenses.

The leadership of some labor unions, especially those with many female members, advocates these items. One mother said, "A woman who has a baby deserves disability pay just as much as a man who has a hernia." (The two "disabilities" are hardly equivalent, but that subtlety is lost in the argument over who pays.) Other unions, however, feel that such coverage of women employees threatens company or union money available to male employees in a time of recession.

None of these advances is won without a struggle. The Equal Opportunity Commission has filed about a dozen maternity leave, class action suits against employers as big as duPont, and many private suits are pending. The city of Philadelphia is defending itself against women workers who want to extend the municipal sick leave policy (20 days per year, 200 days maximum per employee term of service) to pregnancy and birth.

A spokesman in the City Personnel Department gave the usual response. "That would be immensely expensive. We won't pay until forced by law. Some women would be entitled to 105 to 180 days. A woman's whole family could be born in that time." This jealous anger corroborates Dr. Salk's belief that *everything* (a broken arm or hernia) is more important to industry and government than is the family and is therefore financed with minimal suspicion.

Many employers fear the women would misuse their sick leave to malinger and that pregnancy and birth would be the start of frequent absences. Such employers should be referred to statistics showing that working mothers do not lose more job time than other employees.

* * *

Here are a few pointers for enlarging the coverage of your present health insurance plan and for choosing new insurance. Generally, there are three kinds of health insurance: "Basic hospital" pays for inpatient hospital costs, tests, x-rays, drugs, etc.; "major medical" pays other fees connected with surgery or sudden illness; "disability income" gives you benefits if you are unable to perform your usual work (although defining "disability" in regard to any particular occupation is always difficult).

1. *Understand your coverage.*

Which outpatient services, like x-rays or lab tests, are covered?

Which inpatient services? You are an inpatient once you have registered at the hospital admitting office, as distinct from the emergency room or the radiology lab. Generally it is best to get diagnostic tests on an outpatient, not inpatient, basis and, if possible, to avoid the hospital by getting them at your doctor's office or a clinic. The reason is that hospitals use their laboratories to cover losses from other departments. You may pay $15 to $25 for an x-ray at a hospital that you could receive elsewhere for $10. Blue Cross coverage, for example, differs from state to state. In some states Blue Cross does pay for doctors' office workups, while in others, these services must be done at the hospital for cost reimbursement.

Must your number of allowable inpatient hospital days per year be apportioned among the whole family?

Are you limited to using only certain doctors or hospitals?

Is there out-of-area coverage?

What is the waiting period for payment of benefits? Before a new policy takes effect?

Which potential complications of pregnancy are specifically mentioned?

What is the deductible for any of these items? Generally, the higher the deductible (what you must pay before the company pays the rest), the cheaper the insurance. A good policy pays "full service benefits minus a deductible." A good ratio is 80 to 20 percent. The company pays 80 percent; you pay 20 percent, above the deductible. This is "co-insurance."

Is the maximum amount for which the company is liable given in days or in dollars ("indemnity basis")? If in dollars, check that the amounts are up to date for rising medical costs. A good wording states the the company will pay "reasonable and customary fees" for the services you need.

2. *Does your coverage include the new baby* in addition to you?

Some plans have clauses that exclude infants until 14 days of age or mother's discharge from hospital. This will not cover hospital nursery charges or any baby emergency equipment, like a respirator.

3. *Request an itemized hospital bill* and examine it.

Did you ever hear about the Phoenix, Arizona, man who, hospitalized for pneumonia in 1970, found himself billed for use of the delivery room? When he checked further, he discovered it was for "delivery of a baby girl"!

You may deliver a baby girl, and you wouldn't want to be billed for pneumonia.

4. *What happens to coverage if you should lose your present job?* Can you convert easily to another contract?

5. *Do husband and wife both work?*

If so, you may be financing some duplicate coverage. If you have two insurance agents, ask how to consolidate your coverage and reduce premiums.

6. *Check cancellation or renewal provisions.*

Policy should be "noncancellable" or "guaranteed renewable." "Renewable at the option of the company" is not safe wording. Investigate special "riders" that look suspicious. For instance, does the policy cover, or refuse, expenses for illnesses contracted within or beyond some time limit? A retroactive clause that refuses payment for new expenses due to "a 3-year pre-existing condition" (an illness that began before 3 years ago) is unwise. A one-year period is safer.

Can the agent promise you that your premiums won't be raised unless everybody's in your group are?

7. *If you apply for new insurance, tell the truth* on your application.

If you fail to report a pre-existing condition, such as diabetes or heart disease in husband or wife, you may get a policy easily. However, if you are hospitalized for pregnancy-related complications due to such conditions, the trouble you will have with your insurance company may give you high blood pressure as well.

Blue Cross and Blue Shield remain the two most populated, if not popular, U.S. health insurance plans, with over 70 million people enrolled individually or through group plans at their companies. Many more participate in newer plans such as Kaiser Permanente in California or HIP (Health Insurance Program) around New York City. These latter plans combine prepayment of premiums with group practice by doctors. They are probably the best contracts so far devised that combine reasonable fees, broad coverage, and some supervision of practice.

For further information on such a prepaid group plan in your area, you can write to Group Health Association of America, Inc., 2121 Pennsylvania Ave., N.W., Washington, D.C. 20005. For detailed and comparative information or statistics on various insurance plans for groups or individuals, write Health Insurance Association of America, 750 Third Ave., New York, N.Y. 10017.

To check on a particular company, look in *Best's Insurance Reports,* a volume in the reference or financial section of many libraries. A good company has a relatively unembattled record for payment of claims and a return rate above at least 50 percent of what it grosses in premiums. Your State Insurance Commissioner is supposed to have public records of legal or administrative action taken against embattled or failing companies.

CHAPTER **18**

Getting the Birth
You Want

LENI SCHWARTZ IS A RESEARCHER IN PSY-chological birth preparation in the New York area. The mother of three grown children, she is a member of the holistic birth movement, begun recently in California. (See Appendix IV.) She organized a childbirth conference I attended in Tarrytown, New York. Her original interest was in architecture and environment as "human spaces." She notes, "The womb is our earliest example."

Her latest work for her Ph.D. thesis involved a project called "Birth Environment." This was a discussion by small groups of couples, all expecting their first child; most were eager to participate. One father concluded, "Lamaze gives technical skills, but this sharing together is really what prepared us."

Leni videotaped each group during the pregnancies and then two months following the births. When she reviewed and edited the tapes, she was surprised.

How did "before" correlate with "after" for all these couples?

She said, "Casually expressed opinions turned out to have surprising relevance to the kind of birth each couple finally experienced. The kind of delivery a couple had was consistent with their fears and fantasies, especially of the women. Carol, for instance, had so many fantasies, terror of the hospital and giving birth, so she gave birth at home but had a 30-hour labor."

By contrast, other couples also learned and prepared carefully but maintained positive ideas about the coming experience. Afterward they made comments such as, "I would push, but then my whole body would push. It was overwhelming!" One father remarked, "I hope we can do it again sometime!" The videotapes showed plainly the joy and success on these parents' faces.

Leni Schwartz's groups were not large, nor did they emphasize any particular method other than Lamaze, but her work does demonstrate the psychosomatic unity of pregnancy and birth as life events. Birth is a celebration of a life for those who know or learn how to make it so.

A "successful birth" is one that invigorates and allows all the participants, including the baby, a dignified and safe experience. The argument of this book is that attention to three crucial factors—careful choice of doctor and medical care, adequate physical preparation, and optimistic attitude—will help you achieve the birth you want.

About 1960 another psychologist, W. R. Rosengren, studied normal women and their doctors to determine the attitudes of both groups regarding pregnancy and to correlate these psychological factors with delivery room difficulties.

He found that a woman's length of labor correlated directly with how she viewed pregnancy and birth (as a normal state or as an illness) and how her physician also viewed them. "With other variables controlled, it was found that the group of women whose perceptions were *non*congruent with those of their obstetricians, in either direction, had a strikingly significantly longer labor—more than 7 hours longer." To me, this does not mean you should do away with doctors or hospitals or have babies at home. It does mean search, question, choose, until you have assembled the *best* of the services your community provides.

If you've waited until 35 for a baby, you are not alone among Americans. Due to educational, feminist, and health reform movements, child birthing and rearing patterns are changing for everyone, especially for older couples. Did you know that at least one-third of all U.S. married couples are now waiting longer to have their first child? That is, the sociology and demography of birth have already changed. In 1950, one-fifth of married women under 30 had never borne children; by 1960, this figure rose to one-fourth. And by 1974, one-third of U.S. married women were waiting until after their thirtieth birthday to have a first child.

For both sexes, this means that the familiar pattern of marriage at 18 or 22, followed quickly by several pregnancies, may be ending. Trends toward smaller families, reliable birth control, day care, higher education and employment for women will continue.

One over-35 parent wrote me, "I've solved the problems of my childhood, and old age hasn't hit yet, so I'm doing pretty well!"

Other parents whom I questioned made similar observations. Judith, 37-year-old Maryland mother of a new baby, wrote: "My husband and I had been married 9 years. I was shocked and he was shocked when I discovered the pregnancy. He attended classes and was with me throughout labor and delivery. My doctor was great at delivery, although we do need alternatives to hospitals. I heard too much about 'delayed pregnancy.'

"I'm an interior designor, and I take the baby to work with me (since she was 3 weeks). I love being a mother —but what a responsibility! I can't speak for the younger woman, but I'm enjoying my baby more than I would if I'd had her earlier."

APPENDICES

APPENDIX I FOODS AND REPRODUCTION

Vitamins	Sources	Has Effects On
A	fish liver oil, beef liver, yellow and green vegetables, milk products	growth, teeth in young, stillbirth, cleft palate, skin, mucus changes, infant eczema
B_1 (thiamin)	cereal grains, wheat germ, seeds, pork	nerve lesions, morning sickness, fertility
B_2 (riboflavin)	milk whey, egg white, liver, kidney, leafy vegetables, legumes	birth defects, fertility, infant eczema, eye disturbances
B_3 (niacin)	liver, yeast, wheat germ	toxemia, fertility, eclampsia,* edema
B_6	yeast, cereal grains, wheat germ, liver	infant convulsions, morning sickness, eclampsia,* toxemia of pregnancy, edema
B_{12}	liver, dairy foods	pernicious anemia, defective digestion
choline	liver, yeast, wheat germ, bran, egg yolk	toxemia, fertility, colostrum

* See definitions, pages 205–208.

folic acid	liver, yeast, green leafy vegetables	birth deformities, abruptio placentae,* anemia, premature birth, toxemia, mother and infant anemia
pantothenic acid	liver, yeast, wheat germ, nuts, seeds, leafy vegetables	fertility
C	citrus fruits, fresh vegetables	infant scurvy, miscarriage, abruptio placentae,* varicose veins, infection, labor
D	sun on skin, cod and halibut oils	rickets (malformed skull, chest, and legs), restlessness, delay in child development, calcium absorption
E	cereal grains, wheat germ, vegetable oil, nuts	fertility, phlebitis, toxemia, miscarriage, oxygen to the fetus, muscular dystrophy, labor
K	intestinal bacteria (helped by yoghurt), green vegetables, liver	excessive bleeding, infant hemorrhage, cerebral palsy
Minerals	*Sources*	*Has Effects On*
calcium	milk, yellow cheese	rickets, bones and teeth
chromium	yeast, liver, corn oil	body sugar tolerance
copper	liver, kidney	anemia in the young

* See definitions, pages 205–208.

iodine	iodized salt, kelp, salt water fish	mental retardation, thyroid hormones, dwarfism, cretinism
iron	pork and beef liver, eggs, wheat germ, yeast, greens	fertility, hemoglobin formation, anemia, brain and nerve formation in infants
magnesium	beans, bran, nuts, peas, whole grains	bones, teeth, birth defects, toxemia
manganese	wheat germ, nuts, bran, green leafy vegetables, liver	mammary gland function, growth retardation, fertility, hyperactivity
potassium	meat, fish, beans, lentils, dried fruit, nuts	rapid growth, neuromuscular irritation, allergies
zinc	nuts, beans, lentils, green leafy vegetables, seeds, yeast, wheat germ	male fertility, abnormality of eyes, brain, sex development

APPENDIX II   PREGNANCY AND BIRTH WORDS

abruptio placentae—premature detachment of a normally situated placenta.

amniocentesis—apiration of fluid from the amniotic sac surrounding the fetus. Done by needle through the mother's abdominal and uterine walls.

amniotic fluid—clear, straw-colored liquid in which the baby floats in the uterus. Amounts to about 3 pints at term when the membranes containing it rupture and birth ensues.

analgesic—drug, gas, or other agent that relieves or reduces pain without causing unconsciousness. Aspirin, Demerol, Nembutal, and atropine are analgesics.

anencephaly—neurologic disorder of the brain; a neural tube defect.

anesthesia—drug, gas, or other agent used to prevent pain. *Local* anesthesia is injected beneath the skin, into muscles or other tissues, or into the spinal canal to desensitize particular areas of the body. An example is Novocain. *General* anesthesia is used to induce sleep. Examples are sodium pentothal, trilene and nitrous oxide gases.

Some types of local anesthesia pertinent to childbirth are *caudal* (placed in nerves of the spinal cord at the base of the spine); low spinal (*"saddleblock"*) that blocks sensation in the lower pelvis and thighs. The difference between saddleblock and other spinals is that the medication used is heavier than the fluid of the spinal canal and sinks to a lower area, rather than distributing vertically throughout the canal. Other examples are *pudendal* (numbs the outside of the vagina and genital area); *paracervical* (numbs the area around the cervix for passage of baby's head and decreases labor sensations); *epidural* (placed in the space lined by ligament and bone external to the dura—a tough membrane covering the spinal cord and brain—rather than in the spinal cord itself).

antepartum period—pregnancy from conception to labor.

Apgar scale—a battery of tests used to determine the health of newborns; named after its developer, Dr. Virginia Apgar.

birth canal—baby's passageway from uterus out through cervix, vagina, vulva.

breech delivery—delivery in which baby is born feet or

buttocks first. Normal delivery is head first with baby's chin on its chest.

cervix—neck or entrance to the womb.

Clomid—fertility drug that stimulates the pituitary gland, which in turn stimulates ovarian follicles to mature and release eggs that would otherwise be retained.

colostrum—"first milk"; a secretion of the breasts before onset of true lactation 2 or 3 days after delivery.

cystic fibrosis—C/F; inherited degenerative disease, probably fatal, that damages lungs and gastrointestinal tract. Happens once in every 1,500 births when both parents have the recessive gene causing it and transmit these genes to the child.

cytology—science of cell life and formation.

dilatation—opening of the cervix prior to expulsion of a child at term.

dominant gene—one of a pair of genes that determine a given trait. Capable of masking the effect of the other gene when both are present in same cell. Can produce a recognizable birth defect.

eclampsia—a major toxemia of pregnancy accompanied by high blood pressure, headache, convulsions, coma. Can be fatal without treatment.

edema—swelling of body tissue caused by retention of fluid in spaces between cells, especially of hands, feet, face during pregnancy.

episiotomy—surgical cut at vaginal entrance made before baby's head passes through.

fetology—new branch of medicine dealing with diagnosis in the unborn infant from 3 months after conception to birth.

gonad—ovary or testes.

gonadotropin—a gonadotropic hormone. In an infertile woman, monthly injections of one form of this hormone can stimulate egg follicles of the ovaries to mature and release several eggs during each cycle.

hematology—science of the blood.

hypertension—high blood pressure. The heart, upon each contraction, is pushing blood through arteries at a pressure greater than 140 mm. as registered on sphygmomanometer equipment (sleeve with bulb and dial placed around your arm).

infertility—inability to produce offspring. A couple is said to be infertile after trying to have a child without success for 2 years. *Sterility* is a term applied only to cases of absolute infertility, indicated by complete failure to produce sperm or egg cells, lack of reproductive organs, etc.

intrapartum period—labor and delivery to one hour after birth.

karyotype—display of an individual's 23 pairs of chromosomes, ordered by size and other specific markings.

meiosis—cell maturation and division to form new cells.

neonatal—pertaining to the period from infant's birth to age 28 days.

neural tube defects—neurologic disorders or deformities of spine or brain, such as spina bifida and anencephaly.

nullipara—woman who has never been pregnant.

palpation—technique by which examining physician feels with his hands for signs that help him determine what is happening inside the body.

para—refers to past pregnancies that have achieved viability. Parity of a woman refers not to the number of times she has been pregnant but to the number of times she has delivered a living child through the birth canal.

pelvic organs—female organs contained within the hollow of the pelvic bones. They include uterus, vagina, ovaries, Fallopian tubes, bladder, rectum.

Pergonal—human menopausal gonadotropin; hormone that directly stimulates ovaries to mature and release egg cells.

perinatal—pertaining to period from 28 weeks of pregnancy to the time when infant is 7 days old.

perineum—tissue surounding rectum and vagina.

PKU—phenylketonuria; inability to digest protein due to an enzyme deficiency.

pitocin—one of the hormones of the pituitary gland; stimulates uterine contractions before and after birth.

postpartum—pertaining to the period after birth of a baby.

premature—pertaining to a baby weighing less than 5½ pounds; pertaining to labor that commences before the thirty-sixth week (ninth month) of pregnancy.

primigravida—a woman pregnant for the first time.

primipara—a woman who has borne one live child.

sonography—use of high-frequency (ultrasound) waves to visualize the developing fetus without radiation danger. Sound waves bounce off the fetus, and the resulting pattern of dots on paper reveals the outline of baby's head and body.

spina bifida—congenital defect of the fetus in which walls of the spinal canal do not fuse properly. Membranes and nerves of the spinal cord (inside the bony spinal column) may push through opening. A neural tube defect.

toxemia—complication of pregnancy associated with high blood pressure, swelling of hands and feet, albumin in urine.

translocation—fusion of parts of all of 2 chromosomes in each body cell, resulting in chromosomal abnormality. The cause of some Down's syndrome in humans.

zygote—fertilized egg after chromosome groups from ovum and sperm have met.

APPENDIX III   USEFUL BOOKS

Pregnancy

Hazell, Lester Dessez. *Commonsense Childbirth*. New York, Putnam, 1969. Sensible, nontechnical book by a mother of 3 children on choosing a doctor, preparing for home delivery, alerting yourself to your body's signals during labor and delivery. Much advice on breast-feeding.

Milinaire, Caterine. *Birth*. New York, Harmony/Crown, 1974. Picture book, interviews with mothers and fathers, practical advice.

Nilsson, Lennart, Ingelman-Sundberg, Axel, and Wirsen, Claes. *A Child Is Born: The Drama of Life before Birth*. New York, Delacorte, 1966. Photo essay on embryology and stages of fetal development.

Genetics

Apgar, Virginia and Beck, Joan. *Is My Baby All Right?* New York, Trident Press, 1972. Detailed discussion of mechanics of heredity, congenital and environmental birth defects.

Gehman, Betsy. *Twins: Twice the Trouble, Twice the Fun*. Philadelphia, Lippincott, 1965.

Kaufman, Sherwin. *New Hope for the Childless Couple: Causes and Treatment of Infertility*. New York, Simon & Schuster, 1970.

Rorvik, David, and Shettles, Landrum. *Your Baby's Sex: Now You Can Choose*. New York, Dodd, Mead, 1970; paperback, Bantam, 1971.

Nutrition

Lappé, Frances Moore. *Diet for a Small Planet*. New York, Ballantine, 1974.

Be a Healthy Mother, Have a Healthy Baby. Emmaus, Pa., Rodale Press, 1973.

Psychology

Chertok, Leon. *Motherhood and Personality: Psychosomatic Aspects of Childbirth*. Philadelphia, Lippincott, 1969.

Colman, Arthur, and Colman, Libby. *Pregnancy: the Psychological Experience*. New York, Herder and Herder, 1971.

Hobson, Laura Z. *The Tenth Month.* New York, Dell, 1972. Novel about a 40-year-old unmarried woman who decides to continue a pregnancy and present the baby as adopted.

Hunt, Bernice, and Hunt, Morton. *Prime Time.* Briarcliff Manor, N.Y., Stein and Day, 1975. Guide to creative ilving for men and women over 40.

Klein, Carole. *The Single Parent Experience.* New York, Avon, 1973. Comprehensive guide, very optimistic.

Shereshefsky, Pauline, and Yarrow, Leon (eds.). *Psychological Aspects of First Pregnancy and Early Postnatal Adaptation.* New York, Raven Press, 1973.

Labor and Delivery

Bradley, Robert. *Husband-Coached Childbirth,* New York, Harper, 1974.

Ewy, Donna, and Ewy, Roger. *Preparation for Childbirth: A Lamaze Guide.* New York, New American Library, 1974. Test, photos, exercises.

Karmel, Marjorie. *Thank You, Dr. Lamaze: A Mother's Experience in Painless Childbirth.* Philadelphia, Lippincott, 1959; paperback, Doubleday. Contrast between French and American birth methods.

Kitzinger, Sheila. *The Experience of Childbirth.* Baltimore, Penguin Books, 1967.

———. *Giving Birth: The Parents' Emotions in Childbirth.* New York, Taplinger, 1971.

Kroger, William. *Childbirth with Hypnosis.* North Hollywood, Calif., Wilshire, 1961, newest edition, 1974. Basic book on this topic. Still needs updating of quoted research and removal of patronizing attitude toward women.

Leboyer, Frederick. *Birth Without Violence.* New York, Knopf, 1975.

Rorvik, David. *Decompression Babies.* New York, Dodd, Mead, 1973.

Tanzer, Deborah, and Block, Jean. *Why Natural Childbirth?* New York, Doubleday, 1972.

Vellay, Pierre. *Childbirth Without Pain,* New York, Dutton, 1960. Thorough discussion of Lamaze techniques, anatomy and physiology of pregnancy and birth.

———. *Childbirth With Confidence.* New York, Macmillan, 1969.

Parenting

Dodson, Fitzhugh. *How to Father.* Los Angeles, Nash, 1973.

Pomeranz, Virginia. *The First 5 Years: A Relaxed Approach to Child Care.* New York, Doubleday, 1973.

Salk, Lee. *Preparing for Parenthood.* New York, David McKay, 1974. Friendly advice from a pediatrician on handling ambivalent feelings, meeting child's emotional and physical needs, changing trends in family life.

Finance and Insurance

Annas, George J. *The Rights of Hospital Patients.* New York, Avon, 1975; E. P. Dutton, 1976. Question and answer handbook by a lawyer. Urges creation of "patient's rights advocates" in hospitals to discuss aspects and alternatives of care *before* they reach malpractice suit proportions.

APPENDIX IV   ADDRESSES

Chapter 4. Genetics

National Genetics Foundation, 250 West 57th St., N.Y., N.Y. 10019.

National Foundation-March of Dimes, P.O. Box 2000, White Plains, N.Y. 10602. Publishes *International Directory of Genetic Services.*

Chapter 6. Infertility

United Infertility Organization, P.O. Box 23, Scarsdale, N.Y. 10583. Hot line telephone number: (914) 723-1687.

New York Fertility Research Foundation, Inc., 123 East 89th St., N.Y., N.Y. 10028.

Chapter 9. Psychology

Dialogue House, 45 West 10th St., N.Y., N.Y. 10011.

Marriage Encounter National Office, 5305 West Foster Ave., Chicago, IL. 60630.

Chapters 15 and 16. Birth Methods

American Society for Psycho-Prophylaxis in Obstetrics, Inc., 1523 L St., N.W., Washington, D.C. 20005. Lamaze method.

ICEA (International Childbirth Education Association), 208 Ditty Bldg., Bellevue, WA. 98004.

American Academy of Husband-Coached Childbirth, P.O. Box 5224, Sherman Oaks, CA. 91413.

American Society of Clinical Hypnosis, 2400 East Devon, Suite 218, Des Plaines, IL. 60018.

Lynne Gordon, Hypnosis Center of New York, 160 West 73d St., N.Y., N.Y. 10023.

Gayle Gaylord Ashby, Hypnosis Consultation and Referral Center, 152 West 58th St., N.Y., N.Y. 10019.

American College of Nurse-Midwives, 50 East 92nd St., N.Y., N.Y. 10028.

Norman Casserley, 523 Cliffside, Columbus, O. 43202.

Ellen R. Cades, Parent & Child, Inc., 12401 Vinton Terrace, Silver Spring, MD. 20906.

Doris Haire, American Foundation for Maternal and Child Health, Inc., 30 Beekman Place, N.Y., N.Y. 10022.

H.O.M.E. (Home Oriented Maternity Experience), 511

New York Ave., Tacoma Park, Washington, D.C. 20012. Supplies information on materials and techniques needed for safe home birth.

Lolly Hirsch, New Moon Communications, Box 3488, Ridgeway Station, Stamford, Conn. 06905. Variety of gynecology self-help and and childbirth materials, including *The Monthly Extract,* a newsletter.

William Stanninger, Institute for Holistic Childbirth, 1627 Tenth Ave., San Francisco, CA. 94122. Trains both teachers and medical personnel in variety of new birth methods, including Dr. Leboyer's techniques. Is establishing a birth clinic for homelike births.

INDEX

Index